How to Insure Your Child's Success in School

How to Insure Your Child's Success in School

Nancy L. Johnson

Mike Murach & Associates, Inc.

4222 West Alamos, Suite 101
Fresno, California 93711
(209) 275-3335

Many thanks to the following companies for allowing us to reprint the materials listed:

Figure 5-1 from ARE YOU MY MOTHER? by P.D. Eastman. Copyright © 1960 by P.D. Eastman. Reprinted by permission of Random House, Inc.

Figures 5-5 and 7-3 reprinted by permission of Hayes School Publishing Co., Inc.

Figure 5-8 reprinted by permission of Modern Education Corporation.

Figure 6-2 reprinted by permission of Child Guidance.

Figures 6-3, 6-5, and 8-2 and the photos of the play tiles, wooden cubes, and parquetry blocks in figure 6-4 reprinted by permission of Playskool, Inc., Chicago, IL 60651.

Figures 7-6 and 8-9 reprinted by permission of Garrard Press.

Figure 8-3 and the photo of the pegboard in figure 6-4 reprinted by permission of Lauri, Inc.

Figure 8-4 reprinted by permission of Fisher-Price.

Library of Congress Catalog Card Number: 82-62372
ISBN: 0-9116-2500-3

10   9   8   7   6   5   4   3   2   1

Contents

Introduction

If your child does well in school, he feels good about himself. He has the confidence to try to learn whatever his teacher asks him to. He increases his skills and is able to achieve at higher and higher levels. He's caught up in a continuing cycle of success.

But for many children, this cycle never starts.

My son, who had seemed so bright and creative in kindergarten, didn't do well in first grade. He couldn't print his letters, he didn't finish his workbooks, and he didn't learn how to read. He hated to go to school. He cried every morning and didn't want to get out of bed.

I was surprised and confused at his inability to learn. I had always loved school and done well. I began to ask myself: What's wrong with him? Why is he failing? What have *I* done wrong? What's wrong in the school? How can I help?

To find the answers, I went to Northwestern University and in 1977 earned a Master of Arts in Teaching degree. For five years I taught in a Chicago city school where I was able to observe teachers and students with a wide range of natural abilities and cultural advantages. Every summer I studied to discover what educational research had concluded about success in school.

This book tells you what I've learned. I'll take you into the classroom, the library, and—most important—the home, to show you how you can begin the cycle of success with your child. I'll share my experiences with school failures and successes ... those of my own children as well as of the children I've taught ... so you'll know what works and what doesn't.

My own children are a boy and a girl in a nationally rated "excellent" suburban school district. In fact, the high school is one of the top 12 public secondary schools in the country. My son's achievement scores place him in the gifted category, and my daughter ranks "high average." I know now that without my help, neither of them would have reached these levels of achievement.

The children I've taught are in the first elementary magnet school in the city of Chicago. The school was set up by the Chicago Board of Education, the federal government, and Northwestern University to attract children to a unique, integrated educational setting. Parents submit their children's names for voluntary busing to the school. Then, a computer selects the students to represent every racial, ethnic, and socio-economic level present on the north side of Chicago.

This means that in every class, 45 percent of the students are white, 35 percent are black, 19 percent are Hispanic, and 6 percent are from other minority groups. Their varied ethnic backgrounds are reflected by 52 languages—Vietnamese, Greek, Romanian, and Armenian, just to name a few. Their economic levels range from those who live in expensive Lake Shore Drive high-rise apartments (an area referred to as the Gold Coast) to those whose homes are in the poor, ghetto high-rise housing project called Cabrini-Green. Their educational backgrounds vary from the child whose parent is a lawyer, teacher, or doctor to the child of the unemployed, unskilled welfare recipient.

The school has nine open classrooms called "pods" with a total enrollment of 1800 students. Each pod has 200 children with several team teachers in an 8,000 square-foot environment. It's a non-graded effort at quality, integrated, individualized education.

My five years of experience in the preschool, kindergarten, and first-grade pods have provided me with a comprehensive look at a diverse school population. My experiences with my own children have helped me see school achievement from the parent's point of view. Together, these experiences have convinced me that 99 percent of all children *can* succeed in school ... if we, as parents, help them do it.

In chapter 1, then, we'll take a look at the research that explains why some children fail and some succeed even though they live in the same neighborhood, have the same teachers, are of the same race or ethnic background, and have parents with similar jobs and earnings. You'll learn how you can help your child no matter what your economic or cultural background. And you'll learn why you should make sure your child acquires one key skill ... the ability to read.

In chapter 2, you'll see how reading is taught today in the schools. You'll find out why 30 percent of our schoolchildren don't learn to read in school at all ... and why your child could be one who won't.

Chapter 3 documents how children learn to read at home on their own, without any instruction. It will explain why some children do and some don't and how your child can be one who does.

The work of Piaget and Montessori is the subject of chapter 4. The theories of this famous psychologist and this renowned teacher changed the schools. When you know about their work with children, you'll know what you need to do to help your child learn easily both at home and at school.

Next, I'll show you how I taught pre-reading skills to ten "unteachable" kindergartners ... skills that resulted in significantly higher IQ scores at the end of the year. In other words, chapter 5 gives you the exact activities that produced results in the classroom so you can use them at home.

While chapter 5 tells you how a teacher raises the skill level of children in a group, chapter 6 gives you more specific, individual ways to help your child at home. Here, you'll learn how you can easily establish an early learning environment that's guaranteed to prepare your preschooler for success in reading ... and in school.

Chapters 7 and 8 follow the same pattern. From the actual classroom account of my work with first graders in chapter 7, you'll see how children begin to read in school so you can use the same activities and the easy formula in chapter 8 to teach your own child.

Chapter 9 tells you how to provide the additional skills and practice your child needs in spelling and reading in the middle grades. Or, if you have an upper-grade child who's failed to learn to read well in the primary years, you can use these exercises to reverse his cycle of failure. I devised and used this program to help my own daughter and a neighbor girl, so once again you can be sure that the activities do produce results.

Basically, then, this is a reading book. But if you really want to insure your child's success in school, you'll give him more than reading skills. That's what the last two chapters are all about. Chapter 10 tells you how to teach your child the kinds of behavior that will enable him to do his best and learn the most throughout his school years. Then, chapter 11 tells you how to keep your child reading and learning.

Everything in this book works. It's been proven in the classroom and in the home. If you follow the step-by-step instructions, you'll insure your child's success in school. Let me know of your results.

Nancy L. Johnson
October 1982
Chicago, Illinois

Before you begin

There's some controversy these days over using masculine pronouns when you're referring in general to a person who could be either male or female ... as I do throughout this book when I talk about "the child." As a working mother with a daughter of my own, I know that those of you with daughters and those of you concerned about women's issues may be annoyed by this.

The fact is, though, English just doesn't have a good set of neuter pronouns to use in such cases. And the "he or she," "him or her," etc., construction gets cumbersome in a hurry. So to keep this book as readable as possible, I've followed the long-accepted practice of using the masculine pronouns whenever I'm not talking about a specific child.

I simply ask you, as you read the book, to always keep your own child—son or daughter—in mind.

IMAL BABIES by Ylla
STORY BY ARTHUR GREGOR
DO Y
23
Since the ferries no longer cross the Bay, the Ferry Building
now houses the World Trade Center.

Chapter 1

What the research says to you

Lisa and Tracy were cousins in my first-grade classroom. Their fathers were brothers and worked in the same plant. The girls lived in the same building, rode the same bus to school every day, and had the same teacher. Yet, at the end of the year, Lisa read on the second-grade level while Tracy had just begun to read.

During the day, Lisa listened attentively and responded with curiosity and interest. She eagerly tried to print her letters and do the exercises in her workbook. In contrast, Tracy was easily distracted and quickly discouraged. She didn't want to write and gave up easily.

Did Lisa come to school with an innate intelligence that enabled her to learn faster? Was a basic personality difference the cause of their uneven achievement? Or was there another reason to explain their differences?

Many times I have seen this disparity repeated. Children of the same race or cultural background achieve differently in school. Children whose parents make the same amount of money produce different results in the classroom. Children of parents of the same educational level do different levels of work.

But rarely do children of the same family vary greatly in their achievement. That's why teachers always ask, "Don't I know your brother?" if he preceded you in their class. They anticipate the same kind of success or failure from other siblings in the same family. But why?

When I went back to school to train to become a teacher, I wanted to find the answer to this question: Why do some children succeed and others fail? I wanted to discover what kind of teacher would produce results. I wanted to know what caused a child to achieve at his optimum level.

I found that thousands of studies have been done to try to determine what factors will predict academic achievement. Many of them were prompted by the Supreme Court's 1954 desegregation ruling. In line with that decision, the federal government wanted to find out how to make the schools equal. It wanted to know what key factors in white schools caused students to succeed. What specific physical resources in the school were responsible for academic achievement? Did, in fact, the school make the difference?

So in the 60s, the government granted funds to scholars in education to find out how children learn, what teaching methods work, what qualifications of teachers count in the classroom. Its grants examined the value of school libraries, language programs, reading workbooks—even the effect of the student's eyeblink on his understanding in reading.

Amid all this educational research, in 1966, James S. Coleman and his committee compiled the most comprehensive study ever done. This *Report on Educational Opportunity in the United States* collected information by questioning nearly 600,000 students in grades 1, 3, 6, 9, and 12 from 4,000 schools across the country. Half of the students who took the test were white; the other half, non-white. The study compared school facilities, urban and rural districts, teacher characteristics, family backgrounds, and student attitudes.

The data disclosed that in the classroom, the teacher matters most—not the physical structure or resources of the school. What's more, the study found it's the teacher's verbal ability—not his or her education or training—that accounts for the student's success. If the teacher clearly communicates concepts and skills, the child will reach higher levels of achievement.

But while the researchers expected to show that differences in *schools* account for differences in achievement, the data didn't back up that premise. Instead, the study turned out to be especially significant for us as parents because the statistics clearly showed that what happens at *home*, before the child comes to school, determines how well he'll do on standardized tests after he's been in school.

In other words, some children come to school with an advantage from home that enables them to do well. Neither the resources of the school nor the characteristics of the teacher reduce the effect of that head start. What's more, the Coleman report revealed that this family influence continues to affect the child's achievement as he goes on in school. And for those who don't have this benefit, the school doesn't bridge the gap.

How does the family cause achievement?

What kind of family background produces achievement? Not surprisingly, the child from a wealthy home scored higher on standardized tests than one from a lower-income family. We generally assume that more educational stimulation occurs in a home where money can provide it.

But the Coleman study examined six other home background characteristics. From the statistics, it found that the two factors that directly affect a child's performance are the level of his parent's education and the amount of reading material in his home. If the parents have a higher education, the number of books, magazines, and encyclopedias in the home increases, and children who come from these environments do significantly better in school.

Now that tells us what factors affect achievement, but it doesn't tell us why or how. What's going on in homes where the parents are well-educated? (These tend to be upper-income homes, too.) What do these parents do with their children that helps them achieve at a higher level? And how does the amount of reading material in the home affect the child's education?

The Coleman study published its results in two volumes of charts, graphs, and technical research language. It didn't answer these questions; it merely stated the facts. Almost immediately, others began re-analyzing the data to find reasons for its conclusions and to make its information more available to the public.

In 1972, Christopher Jencks wrote *Inequality: A Reassessment of the Effect of Family and Schooling in America*. It represents the work of the Center of Educational Policy Research at Harvard University, and it took the Coleman report one step further.

In the six years following publication of the Coleman study, several educators had suggested that inherited intelligence causes children of educated parents to do better in school. But that's not what Jencks found. He states that "cultural attitudes, values, and taste for schooling play an even larger role than aptitude and money" in achieving academic success. He thinks that middle-class parents transmit their feelings about education to their children and this matters more than the natural ability of the child or the amount of money in the home.

To illustrate, Jencks notes that the average upper middle-class child will go to school four years longer than the average lower-class child. Why? He says it's because economically successful parents value education as a way to get higher income after graduation. As a result, they teach their children the skills they need to do well in school. And when children have success, they enjoy school more and feel better about themselves so that they want to go on in school. Then too, these parents encourage their children to stay in school even if they don't do well and don't like it. Since they believe education is important for future job success, they help their children overcome their negative feelings about school. Finally, Jencks believes that these children set higher goals for themselves because they feel this pressure from home to continue their education. They know their parents expect them to do well, so they fulfill those expectations.

But how do parents develop these values and attitudes in their children? How do they transmit these positive feelings about education? And, again, how does having a lot of reading material in the home affect achievement?

Two separate investigations conducted between 1961 and 1971 indicate that language is a critical factor in the growth of a child's feelings about school. These studies show how differences in language patterns between middle- and lower-class homes prepare ... or fail to prepare ... a child to do well. They tell us how we can use this information to insure our child's success in school.

Language is critical

When Basil Bernstein, an educational sociologist from the University of London, taught school in a working-class neighborhood, he tested his students and found they scored much lower on a language test than they did on a nonverbal intelligence test. These results showed that his students had more ability than the language tests indicated.

Bernstein thought that the home environment accounted for this discrepancy. He compared the language of middle- and lower-class students and discovered an important difference: the child of the middle class learns to produce and understand two kinds of speech, while the child of the lower class learns only one. Bernstein calls these two sets of language, "codes." He defines one as "restricted" and the other, "elaborated."

Both classes use the restricted code—the informal, general, easily understood speech of everyday life. This is the fast, fluent talk between family members where each person understands the frequently repeated expressions of the other. It consists of limited vocabulary and short, simple sentences; it depends on gestures and body language for understanding.

But only the middle class uses the elaborated code. This is the abstract, analytical language of the school. Its vocabulary expresses more explicit meaning, and its sentences are more complicated.

Parents of the middle class use the elaborated code to socialize the child, to discipline him, to communicate their needs and feelings. Instead of giving brief commands, they explain, justify, and generalize. Rather than order the child to "be quiet," they explain they "can't hear the television when you make so much noise." Rather than direct the child to "stop," they ask him to "go into the other room" or "play with your doll instead of the drum." They give options and explanations that cause the child to think, evaluate, and choose.

Well-educated parents not only use both codes in their daily speech. They also read to their child, which introduces him to the unusual sentence structure and varied vocabulary of books. If a child hears only the restricted code of everyday speech, he comes to the classroom with a limited understanding of words. But if he also hears the language of books, he's ready to listen to his teacher's more complicated sentences and new vocabulary.

Thus, when the middle-class mother and father expose their child to both kinds of language, they prepare him for the school environment. Dr. Bernstein says, "If a child is to succeed as he progresses through school, it becomes critical for him to possess, or at least to be oriented towards, an elaborated code."

During the same period that Dr. Bernstein noted these class language differences, Dr. Robert Hess and Dr. Virginia Shipman conducted their own research at the Urban Child Center at the University of Chicago. Their studies on maternal teaching styles illustrate Dr. Bernstein's theory with a clearer message for parents.

They designed research to study how middle-class and lower-class mothers differ in their ways of teaching their children. They wanted to find out how some mothers help their children learn more than others.

In one experiment, Drs. Hess and Shipman selected 160 mothers and their four-year-old children for participation. The mothers ranged from college-educated professionals to unskilled workers.

For the study the participants came to the laboratory, where the mothers were asked to teach their children how to sort blocks by two characteristics: size and a marking on the top. The children were to divide the blocks into four groups: (1) tall and marked by an X; (2) short and marked by an X; (3) tall and marked by an O; (4) short and marked by an O.

The researchers made certain the mothers understood how to do the sorting themselves but deliberately avoided giving the mothers any directions on how to explain the sorting procedure to their children. Each mother had to use her own way to teach her child to accomplish the sorting of the blocks. The mothers had to motivate their children to sort the blocks, give clear instructions on what to do, and keep them motivated to complete the task.

The results were predictable. Over 60 percent of the middle-class children divided the blocks correctly compared to 33 percent of the lower-class children. But in their observations, Hess and Shipman noticed two striking differences in the teaching styles of the mothers.

First, the more successful mothers were more specific about their directions. They were better organized and clearly put into words what they wanted the child to do while they showed him how to do it. The mothers of the children who didn't learn merely told the child to watch them. For example, read the following excerpt from a successful mother:

> Wait a minute, Johnny. You have to look at the block first before you try to find where it goes. Now, pick it up again and look at it—is it big or small? ... Now, put it where it goes.

Contrast that with the following example of a non-successful mother:

> That doesn't go there—you're just guessing. I'm trying to show you how to do this and you're just putting them any old place. Now pick it up and do it again and this time don't mess up.

The successful mother gives logical steps to follow. She tells her child to look at the block, then to decide its size, and finally to put it in the appropriate group. She doesn't assume that he understands what he's expected to do.

Second, the researchers noted that the mothers who relied on praise and encouragement to motivate their children were more successful than those who were critical and threatening. Praise motivates the child to do the task, rewards him when he finishes it, and makes the task into a pleasant experience. Mothers who command and try to control cause the negative association of annoyance and anger with the task.

The following excerpt from a successful mother illustrates the supportive way she motivates her child to finish the sorting:

> Now, we can't stop now, Johnny. Mrs. Smith wants me to show you how to do this so you can do it for her. Now if you pay close attention and let Mommy teach you, you can learn how to do it and show her, and then you'll have some time to play.

Compare it with the threatening tone of the unsuccessful mother in this passage:

> Now you're playing around and you don't even know how to do this. You want me to call the lady? You better listen to what I'm saying and quit playing around or I'm gonna call the lady in on you and see how you like that.

The successful mother not only gives her child step-by-step directions that enable him to sort the blocks. She praises and encourages him. When her child receives the positive feedback, he enjoys learning. He wants to continue the task until he completes it. Meanwhile, his mother indicates that she expects him to finish when she promises another reward—time to play—if he does.

We begin to see the differences in homes that prepare a child to do well in school. If the parents use school language and read to their child, if they praise and reward, if they give clear directions and set definite long-term goals for achievement, their child will do better.

But what about the child whose parents don't do these things ... especially if he's from a poor, less-educated family? How can he expect to have success? Is there any way to overcome the effects of the home?

Reading offsets family background

In 1978, the International Reading Association conducted a study that looked at individual scholastic performance in two culturally and economically different countries—England and India. And it concluded that one skill—knowing how to read—will make up for the negative effects of family background. In fact, it singled out reading as the all-important factor in school success.

How did the researchers come to this conclusion? They measured the effects of the home influences we've already talked about—the development of language and thinking skills, the wealth of the family, and the educational level of the parents—plus the effect of reading skill on success in physics, chemistry, and biology.

As one result of their research, they found that a person needs language and thinking skills to learn how to read. Both begin to develop in the home, and the child who comes from a home that provides an environment for learning these skills does have an advantage in school.

But when the researchers measured achievement in the sciences, they learned that the child who understood what he read had the greatest success. In both the industrialized and the Third-World nation, the children who read well performed better on tests and in practical work, too. What's more, if their reading level went up, their performance in science also went up. Their social class and family background had little or no relationship to their achievement. Only their ability to read affected their performance.

The authors conclude that no teacher is more important than the reading teacher. If a child knows how to read well, he'll perform well in the content areas. He'll gain the vocabulary, language, and thinking abilities he needs to be able to understand and use knowledge in other subjects. He'll have the one skill that will guarantee his success in the classroom.

In school, the child who reads well uses his ability to solve word problems in mathematics, to learn historical facts and geographical data, to master scientific terms and principles. He uses his knowledge of words and sentence structure to write themes and essays. He uses the verbal skills he acquires as he reads to express himself clearly in the classroom.

The more he reads, the better he develops his communication skills. His vocabulary grows to enable him to understand the words and ideas of famous thinkers. His mind stretches to absorb the messages of history and the literature of all countries. He uses this knowledge to solve problems creatively. He becomes an outstanding student.

What does this mean to you?

What does the research say to you? How can you be sure your child will have success in school?

No matter what the economic or cultural circumstances of your home, you can insure his achievement if you see to it that he reads. Whether you make very little money or are fluent in English, whether you have a large family or live in the inner city, if you are sure that your child knows how to read, you can be sure he'll do well in school.

The following case history shows you how it can be done:

My brother and I have always been high achievers. We are both college graduates and have been successful both in school and at work. Yet our parents did not graduate from high school. They were second-generation Americans with limited language skills, and they didn't have a lot of money. How did they do it?

First, they had high hopes for us. They wanted us to graduate from college, and they communicated that message to us in many different ways. Every time they told us about their childhood and their own hopes and dreams, they pointed out how important it was to have an education. They were sure that if they'd had more education, their lives would have been different. Every time they insisted we go to school when we didn't want to, they told us that school learning was valuable. Every time they praised us for doing well in school, they showed us that they cared.

They communicated the value of education in other ways, too. For example, we didn't have many clothes or toys, but we did have a stand-up chalkboard with the alphabet and numbers across the top. My mother had us practice writing the letters every morning. She sat with us and kept us company. When we did it right, she hugged us and showed us how happy it made her. She played school with us and made it seem like fun. She told us again and again that we were very smart and that it was important for us to do well in school.

Second, our parents taught us the value of language and of books. My mother was always self-conscious about her grammar. She read books like *How to Increase Your Vocabulary* and *Words are Power*. She pointed out that educated people spoke differently. She created an awareness in us to listen carefully to how people speak and to try to talk the same way. She never let us use baby talk and made us use the right word to express ourselves.

She showed us she believed in the power of the written word, too, when she read *How to Write Better Letters* and *How to Write, Speak, and Think More Effectively*. She told us she wished she could understand the language of books. She showed us that if we could read, we would be able to find answers to our questions.

My dad worked long hours and didn't have much time to read, but he talked to us about what he did read. He said *The Saturday*

Evening Post and the daily newspaper were his college education—that learning should be a lifelong process, even though many people stop learning when they leave school. He said that knowledge is current. It changes and requires that you read to keep up with those changes.

My parents also encouraged an interest in reading by making sure we had books available. We didn't have much extra money, but when a neighbor sold encyclopedias, my parents bought us a set. For our birthdays and Christmas, my grandmother and uncle always gave us books. And for entertainment, we went to the library. (Of course, we didn't have television.)

When we were little, my mother read to us every day, the same books over and over until we'd memorized them. (As we'll see later on, this was a key factor in our learning how to read.) We looked forward to these times when we could step into the world of make-believe. We looked forward to the pleasure of the same stories.

We learned how to read with little effort, so school was always very easy and pleasant for us. We listened because the teacher talked about the same kinds of things we had read about in our books. Our teachers liked us because we paid attention and did well. They praised us for our successes.

We did our work quickly because we could read and understand it. In our school if you finished your work, you could read whatever you wanted. We read books that introduced us to people and places that expanded our views and knowledge about life. We satisfied our curiosity about the world when we read *The Book of Knowledge* and the encyclopedias. We turned to books when we wanted to find out how to do something and when we wanted to be entertained.

Reading became a pleasure *and* a tool for learning. The more we read, the more our vocabularies grew and the better we did in class. We were interested and eager to learn because books stimulated our curiosity. We wrote more expressively and with better spelling and organization because we read a lot. We loved school and surpassed our peers from wealthier, more educated families in math, history, science, geography, and English.

We never knew what we would be when we grew up. We just knew we would go to college and do well ... and we did. Our parents prepared us for this success when they told us what they expected from us and what we needed to do to realize those dreams. They gave us skills when they taught us the value of language and prepared us to read well.

You can do this for your child, too. If you know what you want your child to achieve, you'll communicate those goals to him. You'll see to it that he learns the skills he needs to succeed. You'll be sure he knows how to read.

Don't underestimate the importance of this responsibility. And don't say to yourself that you should leave it to the schools ... that it's their job, not yours. As you'll see in the next chapter, that attitude could lead to your son or daughter being labeled a "disabled reader" ... one of those who makes up the 30 percent of our schoolchildren who never learn to read well.

Chapter 2

Why 30 percent of our children don't learn to read in school

The dark-haired young teacher picked up the chalk and wrote on the board, "words." She turned to the kindergarten children watching her with close attention and said, "What does that say?" The silence told her that no one had any idea. Enthusiastically, warmly, smilingly, she encouraged them to "take a guess. Tell me, what do you think it could be?" Still no one had an answer (or a guess).

This kind of behavior in the classroom is supposed to stimulate interest in learning to read, but in reality, it confuses children. It teaches them that reading is a guessing game, and the child concludes that if he's lucky, he'll have success. If he's not lucky, he needn't try.

Children come to school curious and questioning, interested and eager to learn. Yet they're also somewhat unsure about school, not knowing why they've had to leave the comfort and security of their homes. They want to do the right thing, but they rarely know why they're in school and what they should be learning. They are told to "be good," and being good means to "be quiet," to "line up," to "wait your turn," and to "share." They learn that it's important to know the "right answer" and that it's all right to guess.

Reading is introduced with mystery and confusion. No one ever says it's easy or it's fun. It's regarded as a difficult skill that not all can master. You have to "work" at it. (Workbooks instead of reading books reinforce this idea about reading.)

For 30 percent of those who come to school not able to read, the mystery and confusion will persist. Why? To find out, let's see how reading is taught in the schools.

Educators believe that because of the complexity of reading and the uniqueness of children, a single teaching method won't work for everyone. They can show that reading is a combination of language, thinking, visual, and auditory skills. We know that children come to school with different family backgrounds and different preparation to learn these skills. Consequently, children learn at different rates. Because of this diversity, educators don't agree on the "right" way to teach reading.

However, in the beginning of formal reading instruction, only one method was used. It aimed to unlock the letter-sound code that is the basis for our language. As a result, the steps to reading mastery were direct and sequential—going from the simple to the complex. Letters were named; sounds were given to the letters; small syllables were sounded out; and finally, words were read.

But teaching was tedious drilling of alphabet names and sounds. Children were bored and restless. Throughout the history of education, teachers have tried to find a way to make learning to read a more pleasant experience.

How schools teach reading

Today, teachers use an "eclectic" approach or several methods to teach your child to read. In 95 percent of the schools in the country, a reading program designed by a publishing company forms the basis of the instruction, and the teacher supplements it with his or her knowledge and ability.

These reading programs try to provide a complete, orderly, step-by-step method of teaching reading to all children. They have manuals that tell the teacher how to introduce the lesson, how to teach the skills, what questions to ask, and what additional exercises to give. They also include filmstrips and transparencies, drill sheets and charts, workbooks and games. Supposedly, all you have to do is open your book, and everyone will learn to read.

The programs are designed to develop the increasingly complex skills of reading from kindergarten through the eighth grade. As a result, they teach reading as a subject by itself ... *not* as an educational tool to be used in other subject areas. To many children today, reading is what you do when you go to reading class and open your workbook.

The most popular and widely used reading programs use the "whole-word" method to teach. This means that children are taught to recognize a word by the way it looks—to look at the shape of the word in its entirety and memorize it. (This is also called the "look-say" method.)

To make memorization a manageable task, the publishing companies use a "controlled vocabulary" in their reading materials. This means that a limited number of words are introduced in each "reader." These words are memorized and then used over and over again in the workbooks and drill sheets. In the first grade, the child learns to recognize on sight about 500 words; in the second grade, from 950 to 1700 words; and in the third grade, from 1900 to 3300 words.

Since children learn at different rates, teachers must give individualized instruction. The publishers' reading programs provide for children's differences by having reading texts that are written at varying levels of complexity. In the beginning of the year, each class is divided into three ability groups. One group has those children who are the most advanced in their reading skills; one has those who are the least advanced; and the third has those who are between the two. The groupings are made to give each child his own time with the teacher as well as to give him group lessons on his skill level.

Every day, then, the teacher takes the children in groups of eight or ten to "read" in the primers on their level. New words are introduced at this time. Usually, the teacher does this by holding up a card with the word and a picture of the word on it. The teacher looks at the word and says it; then the children look at the word and say it.

Usually, the words are distinctly different, so they're easy to recognize by sight. In one beginning series, *Bill, lad, runs, hides, Jill, and, rides, can, this, is, here, not, Ben, a, duck, Ted, Nan, look, at, said, the, park, will, get, we, help, stop, yes,* and *no* are the words taught in Book 1. (Yes, these 29 words are the only ones in the entire book!)

Then the child returns to his seat to write the word and perhaps color a picture of it. The workbook may ask him to choose the word that matches the picture. Or it may ask him to draw a line from the word to the picture. Sometimes he must write the word in the blank that matches the picture.

Phonics instruction, or teaching the sounds for the letters, in a reading series is often done by records and audio-visual filmstrips and tapes instead of the systematic drills that were part of the early days of teaching children how to read. The series also use games and puzzles to develop an awareness of the letter-sound relationships.

To learn these relationships, the children don't have to know the names of the letters. Instead, they're taught to hear the similarity in the beginning sounds of words. Usually, this is done as follows: The teacher will say a word; then, the child must give a word that begins with the same sound. For example, if the teacher says *silly*, the child should respond with a word beginning with the s-s-s sound, such as *sun* or *Sam*.

In another exercise, the teacher will say a group of words. The child must listen for a specific sound and raise his hand when he hears a word beginning with that sound.

Another way to teach reading

Although published reading programs form the basis for reading instruction in the classroom, teachers use other ways to help children learn to read. Many educators have noted that children easily learn words they choose themselves. For example, they remember without difficulty words that have special personal meaning, such as their own names, *Mother*, *Daddy*, *love*, and *Santa Claus*. Knowing this, teachers try to use a child's own vocabulary to teach him to read.

This method is called the language-experience approach to reading. It's used most often in beginning instruction to interest the child and to supplement the publisher's reading program. With this technique, the teacher writes stories on the chalkboard or on chart paper that the children dictate in their own language. For example, after a field trip or special program in the auditorium, children usually write about their experience in a group activity. With them settled in front of the chalkboard, the teacher prints their own "story." A typical one follows:

The Farm

Today we went to the farm. We saw pigs, cows, chickens, horses, goats, and ducks. We saw corn growing in the field and big pumpkins on the ground. Jim was our guide. We had a good time.

These "stories" are typed and distributed to each member of the class. Then, the teacher points out the plurals, pronouns, verb tenses, and rhyming words in them.

This method intends to teach the connection between speech and print—to show children that everything you can say, you can write and then read. Basically, though, it teaches reading the same way the published reading programs do, through the memorization of whole words. The main difference is that the words come from the children's dictation rather than from any books.

Why these methods don't work

Why don't these methods teach all children to read? They make learning sound so pleasant and easy. The publishers' programs are expensive, beautifully illustrated, colorful, and individualized. They give full directions to the teacher. They cover eight grades. Everyone learns at his own pace on his own level of ability.

Why don't they work? Simply stated, these methods fail because they don't give clear messages to the child about what he needs to know to be able to read. From my work with children, I think that learning to read is easy. I believe there are certain definite skills to be mastered. When you know them so that they're automatic responses, you can read anything.

The trouble is, educators don't all agree on what these skills are. For example, some think it's not necessary to learn the alphabet while others feel it's essential. They don't all agree on how we read. Some think we read whole words as they relate to the context of the sentence, and others (including me) argue that we decode words, letter by letter. They don't all agree on a definition of reading. Some think it's a perceptual skill, some see it as purely a language skill, and still others view it as information processing. As a result of this confusion, educators can't agree on a way to teach reading to all children.

Prospective teachers learn in college that reading is the most important subject they can teach. But they're only required to take one or, at the most, two courses in reading for graduation. They learn that reading requires many separate skills. But they're taught that these skills are difficult to master. They learn the statistics of reading failures. They expect that many students won't learn to read well. They go into the classroom confused about how to teach reading and prepared to have children fail.

As a result, many teachers depend on reading programs to tell them what to do. They think that if they do what the manual says, the child will learn to read. When he fails to read well, they look for other explanations. They've been taught there are many reasons for failure.

Sometimes they think the child has developmental problems. Perhaps he's not emotionally mature. Later, he'll understand. Or, perhaps when he can print better, he'll be able to read better. Or, as he gets older, he'll be more interested and pay attention. Then, he'll understand.

If he comes from a poor home, they think it's because he hasn't had enough cultural stimulation. Perhaps after he goes on more field trips, sees more plays, and has more time in the classroom, he'll have a better foundation for learning. Then, he'll start to read.

If he comes from a home where the parents don't speak English as their first language or if the parents are illiterate, the teachers think the student needs more language training. Perhaps when the child talks better, he'll understand.

Sometimes they think the child will do better in a different publisher's reading program. Perhaps if they start him in a new program, he'll begin to read.

Unfortunately, changing from one program to another usually doesn't help much because the programs themselves reflect the confusion in education about reading. Most of them use the whole-word method with the incidental teaching of the letter-sound relationships. But publishers haven't tested these materials. They haven't proved that their programs will teach every child who uses them to read.

Why doesn't the whole-word method work? Obviously, you can't memorize every word that you'll encounter in reading. When the child is limited to reading only the words he has memorized, he's limited in what he can read.

He finds he can read only the materials in reading class. All of the fun of reading cereal boxes, street signs, magazines, and newspapers is denied him because he has no way of figuring out unfamiliar words. He can't divide words into syllables because he hasn't been taught to look at separate parts of words. His eyes haven't been trained to move across the page from one letter to the next; instead, they move from one word to the next. So as the words get longer, he has no way to help him divide them into parts he can read ... even though it gets harder and harder to memorize all the words he's supposed to know.

Not being able to remember all the words frustrates the child. Often, when reading in class, the teacher will say, "What do you think it is?" Not having any skills to help him, the child guesses. When he guesses right, he concludes that reading is a guessing game.

Soon he begins to read by looking at the first letter of each word and guessing the words he doesn't remember. As the years go by and the number of words he should remember increases, he guesses more. Then he's told he needs to read faster, so he speeds up. Now he adds words that aren't there and skips words that are there to make his guessing right.

Most of the time these children are able to complete their workbooks because the vocabulary in them is limited and it's easy to guess the answers. When the parents come for the conference, the teacher tells them the child is progressing. "He's finished Book I and is now working in Book II." But completing levels in a reading program does *not* mean gaining mastery of reading skills.

The result is that most parents aren't aware their child isn't learning how to read until third or fourth grade. By then, years have been wasted in practicing whole-word memorization. The pattern has been set for failure in school. For without reading ability, the child can't achieve success in other subjects.

Many of these children are overlooked. They're able to read enough to get by. They're often called auditory learners—children who get information better by hearing it than by seeing it. Some are finally labeled "disabled" readers. Somehow they can't learn to read.

Of course, they can't write very well either. They have trouble spelling. They can't sound out words to spell them because they've never been taught these skills. They don't know when to use capital letters or how to punctuate properly.

Here again, the workbooks aren't much help because they don't require children to write very much. Most of the time, children are asked to circle or underline a word. As they progress in the program, they fill in the blank by writing one word. But they aren't often asked to write creative stories. They need more writing practice.

What a good teacher does

Seventy percent of the children in our schools learn to read with any teaching method. Some are taught with a reading program that does stress the letter-and-sound relationships. Some—especially those who have help from their parents or older siblings—figure out these relationships by themselves. And some have good teachers—teachers who make sure they learn how to read, no matter what reading program the school is using.

A teacher who is a good reader knows that reading is a decoding process. Each letter or combination of letters stands for a sound. Words are composed of sound units. Thoughts are expressed in groups of words. If you know the code, you can read anything.

These teachers stress the importance of being able to recognize the letters and to know the sounds the letters represent. They insist that the child learn these relationships. In short, they give clear messages on what to learn.

At the same time, these teachers read to the children regularly. They use books that the children enjoy, and they read them in such a way that the stories come alive. They do this to show their students that reading is fun. They do it because they know it motivates the children to want to learn to read the stories on their own. And they do it because they know books help develop good oral vocabularies so when the children do learn to read, they'll understand what they're reading.

The good teachers help children develop their reading skills in gradual and sequential steps. They start the child reading with the small words that are part of his daily vocabulary. They show him how he can learn very easily. They show him that it's fun to play with words. They show him the connections between talking and writing and reading.

They give lots of repetition. They know that children need to do the same thing over and over again until it becomes automatic. In reading, they need to recognize letters and then associate a sound with each letter. In writing, they need to practice copying letters and then words.

The good teachers make every lesson a reading lesson. In art, social studies, science, and even math, they introduce new words. They have the children label drawings, put together books, and make calendars and maps.

In short, they show the children how language relates to everything they do. They use all the classroom activities—even those in seemingly unrelated subjects—to demonstrate the connection between talking, listening, writing, and reading. They treat the entire communication process as a whole so the children can develop skills in all these areas at the same time.

This is the way reading should be taught. Then, it should be used as an educational tool.

It should be used to learn the beauties and complexities of the language. Reading widely increases the ability to read. It gives practice with many different words. Reading skills should be improved not through published programs, but by reading great literature and history.

Children who read only the compositions in their reading series practice only a limited sight vocabulary. Those with problems in the fifth and sixth grade know only *said* and *asked*. They've never read *reproached* or *rebuked* or *grumbled* or *murmured*. They've had experiences with only the simplest sentence structure. When words are in different positions, they're unable to get the meaning.

That's because reading programs don't teach reading. Teachers do. The teacher is the key factor in the classroom because he or she directs the focus of the activities to one learning goal. Teachers need excellent verbal skills to develop good grammar, vocabulary, and writing skills in their students. They need to have the knowledge and ability to supplement whatever reading programs their school uses so that their students actually learn how to read.

What does this mean to you?

You can be your child's reading teacher. You can best prepare your child to learn to read by giving him experiences that provide a foundation for skill development. When he goes to school, you can direct his learning by supplementing his classroom education. As he progresses through the grades, you can be sure that he knows how to read well.

It doesn't require a lot of time or energy. As we'll see in the next chapter, it can be a natural part of your growing relationship with your child. I urge you not to leave this important skill to the variability of conditions of the school.

Chapter **3**

How young children learn to read at home

At the end of the last chapter, I said that you could be your child's teacher and make sure he knows how to read. I wouldn't be surprised, though, if you're not convinced. After all, parents—like too many children and teachers—have been led to think of reading as a difficult, mysterious subject that not everyone can master. We've been told that our child must be "ready" to read before he can be taught. When we ask about this "readiness," we get vague explanations about skill development and emotional maturity. We also get the feeling we won't be able to tell when he's ready. All in all, it seems like reading is a subject that must be taught in schools by professionals.

The fact is, though, many children start school already knowing how to read. How do they learn? What elements in their homes prepare them to read?

Most of the studies that have been done in educational research have not provided any empirical evidence to point the way to definite methods of achievement. In other words, there's very little conclusive proof that if you do this, then that will result. Dolores Durkin has done one of the significant research efforts that does, however, offer real insight into what factors in the home contribute to achievement in reading. And while many other studies have been done since, few have paid attention to the child who knows how to read when he comes to school. In my research, I found Durkin's work unequalled in its implications for parents.

The California study

While a member of the University of California faculty, Dolores Durkin did some research that required her to observe often in a first-grade classroom. Among the pupils she observed was a girl who could read on the fourth-grade level although she hadn't had any previous instruction. Curiosity about how this child had learned to read before she came to school led Dr. Durkin to conduct the two long-term studies that are described in her book, *Children Who Read Early.*

In 1958, she chose Oakland, California as a city large enough to provide a fair sample for the first study. During the first two weeks of school, she used standardized reading tests to find the 49 children who already knew how to read among the 5,103 first-grade pupils in the school district. The scores of these early readers ranged from that of an average reader in the first grade, fifth month to that of an average reader in the fourth grade, fifth month.

The backgrounds of these early readers did not predict their achievement. They didn't all have outstanding IQ's—a factor traditionally thought to be necessary for early reading to occur. Average IQ range is between 90 and 110, and 17 of the 49 early readers had scores in this category. The rest ranged up to 161, with the average for the group at 121. They didn't come from backgrounds of wealth—another factor associated with achievement in learning, as we saw in chapter 1. In fact, 27 came from blue-collar families, and only 7 came from the upper middle class. They didn't come from families with high educational levels. Ten of the 49 families were bilingual; 3 of the mothers could not read English. They were culturally mixed. There were 26 Caucasians, 12 blacks, and 11 Orientals. There were 20 boys and 29 girls.

Dr. Durkin wanted to find out what characteristics in the homes of these children were similar and would give a formula for classroom teachers to improve beginning reading instruction. What she found in her research has equal value to parents who want their children to read and do well in school.

Dr. Durkin gave each family a questionnaire and conducted interviews with the parents and children to find out how the children learned to read. In addition, she selected the early readers who had the highest and lowest IQ's and those with the highest and lowest reading scores at the beginning of first grade for in-depth study. From these selected case studies and the personal interviews, a picture of the home environment for early reading began to emerge.

Parents were asked to select personality characteristics that described their child. All of the children were depicted as curious, persistent, and perfectionist. They were considered to be competitive and to have good memories. They asked lots of questions ... and the significant part is that their families took time and answered them.

Why is that significant? Because immediately it became clear that none of the early readers began to read "all by himself." Every one of them had help.

Eleven of the 49 children in the study had parents who definitely set out to teach them to read. Five of the mothers did so because their children showed a lot of interest in learning. One father had an older child who had found it difficult to learn to read in school, and he wanted to prevent the younger child from having trouble. Only one of the parents was a former teacher, while four of the eleven said they simply responded to their children's questions and taught them because they felt that knowing how to read would help them do well in first grade.

As for the other 38 children, their own curiosity and persistence determined the amount of help they received from a parent or relative in learning how to read. Several had older brothers and sisters who played school with them. For two of them, a grandma and an aunt along with the parent answered their questions about printed words and numbers. For some others, a friend stimulated their interest and helped them to learn words.

How often was this help given? For 21 of the children, it was the same time every day—after a favorite television program or when the other children were doing their homework. For the other 28, it was spontaneous and less often—on rainy days, after a trip to the library, or when both parent and child were interested.

These children liked to scribble, and they advanced from scribbling to drawing people and objects. Next, they became very interested in letters and wanted to know how to print. In 37 of the 49 families, the parents helped their children learn the letters of the alphabet. In some of the homes, the children had alphabet stencils to use for tracing letters.

But every one of the 49 children in the study had a chalkboard in the home. Many of these were the kind that had the alphabet at the top, which may have prompted the desire to print. For some children, the chalkboard had belonged to an older child in the family and that could have aroused an interest in writing. For many of the children, it was merely a small, variety-store lapboard that gave them the opportunity to practice. In all cases, however, the children used these chalkboards to learn how to print letters and then words.

Words ... the children were fascinated by them. Very early they began asking questions about written words on signs, canned goods, storefronts, toys, newspapers—wherever they saw words. And help consistently came in the form of someone telling them what the word was.

In the homes there were plenty of picture dictionaries, alphabet books, and school workbooks and discarded readers that belonged to older brothers and sisters. If these siblings were doing their homework, the early readers were right there wanting to know what they were doing. And again, they were told. Words were identified for them, and many times they were told the sounds for the letters.

Some of the early readers had coloring books with simple one-word labels. For example, the picture to color would be an apple with the word *apple* underneath. Many of the coloring books had simple directions on how to color the picture, such as "Make the hat red." Some children had games that required them to match the pictures with the words. In short, they saw lots of words they could link directly with objects.

Most important, all of the parents and many of the older siblings read to the early reader. And they read the same story again and again until the child had memorized it.

Their reading styles contributed to the early reading of their children. One mother reported she read to her child so that the pages could be seen. Most of the parents put their finger under the words as they went along so the child saw a clear connection between the written and the spoken word.

Definitely, then, there were similar characteristics in the homes of these early readers. But the questions for Dr. Durkin now were: Why don't more children learn to read before first grade? What's going on in their homes? Are their preschool experiences alike or different? Do the personalities of early readers differ from those who don't learn to read before school?

The New York study

Her second longitudinal study was done in New York City between 1961 and 1964. Before first grade began, 4,465 students in 40 schools in Manhattan, Queens, Brooklyn, and the Bronx were tested to find out if any of them could already read. When 157 children proved to be early readers, 30 were randomly selected and matched by sex and IQ scores to 30 non-readers in their classrooms. This time the average IQ of both readers and non-readers was 132, which is in the superior range of the intelligence scale. (Remember, average is between 90 and 110.)

Again, personal interviews using a questionnaire were done with the families in both groups to gather the data needed to compare the preschool experiences of the children. At this time Dr. Durkin asked about family income and education. Since the children had been chosen from many schools in New York City, the two groups turned out to be fairly evenly matched in both social and economic levels, so we can assume that the wealth and education of the families did *not* cause early reading to occur.

In all but 5 of the 60 interviews, only the mother was present; most of the fathers were away at work. At the time, it seems that mothers played the key role in preparing the child to read. But we have to wonder if that still holds true today, when fathers are taking a more active role in parenting. From my own experience, I must say that more mothers come to parent conferences and parent meetings, but most of them strongly express the father's interest and concern. And many fathers do come, either alone or with the mothers, to show that they care. These fathers tell me that they read to their children and try to help them learn letters and words. In Durkin's study, though, the influence of the fathers wasn't as readily apparent as that of the mothers.

From the interviews, some very significant statistics came forth. Eighty-three percent of the mothers of the early readers described themselves as reading more often than the average adult compared to 33 percent of the mothers of the non-readers. (The "average adult reader" was defined as one who reads newspapers, magazines, and occasionally a book.) It's important for the parent to be a model of the behavior he or she seeks in the child.

Not surprisingly, all the early readers were read to at home compared to 73 percent of those who did not learn to read before they entered school. And when the parents read to them, 80 percent told their children what the words were when they asked, while only 41 percent of the parents of the non-early readers did. As in the first study, it was reported that the same story was read over and over again until the child had memorized it.

One hundred percent of the parents of the children who learned to read before going to school thought parents should give help with reading skills to preschoolers, while 50 percent of the parents of the non-readers did not agree. The latter felt that such teaching would interfere with school instruction and result in confusion or boredom. Several had been cautioned by teachers of older siblings not to give any reading lessons at home.

Not one mother of the early readers characterized herself as being "too busy" to take time with her child. These mothers freely answered questions about words and frequently went beyond and told the sounds of the letters. They didn't feel they were teaching; they felt they were merely responding to their children. And they didn't think of this as interfering with the school's job as the mothers of the non-early readers did.

What about the characteristics of the children themselves? In both groups, they were described by the parents in similar terms. "Curious," "competitive," "persistent," and "possessing a good memory" were applied to all the children.

The early readers differed from the non-readers, though, by liking to play alone and without toys. They occupied themselves with quiet games or spent their time coloring or writing or talking to themselves. When asked about television viewing, the parents of the early readers reported that their children spent less time watching television than the non-early readers.

All of the children were early scribblers and were interested in learning how to print their names. But 83 percent of the early readers had paper and pencils available to them in the home compared to 18 percent of the non-early readers. And more parents of early readers gave help with printing.

The long-term achievement

The implications from these studies for parents and the home environment we create are many. But it's also important to know the long-term achievement that resulted from being an early reader. The New York study kept comparisons over a three-year period; the California records cover six years. Because these two studies observed the accomplishments of children over long periods of time, their findings about the positive effects of early reading cannot be denied.

For the brightest students in the studies, knowing how to read before first grade was an educational advantage that never diminished. Fifteen of the 49 early readers in the California study were double-promoted because of the combination of their high intelligence and reading ability. Their average achievement at the end of the six years was significantly higher than that of classmates of the same IQ who had one more year of instruction in reading.

Eight of the 30 early readers in the New York study were double-promoted. However, none of the 30 non-early readers was accelerated. After three years of school instruction in reading, the average reading scores of those who were double-promoted exceeded by 2.3 years the average scores of the non-early readers with whom they were matched.

Of equal value to parents, however, is the finding that the advantage of learning to read before school was greatest for the child of lower intelligence. The California study showed that the early readers with lower IQ's started out ahead of non-readers of similar intelligence and held that lead throughout the six years of the research. Dr. Durkin thinks this head start in reading gave them more time for the repetition and practice they needed to achieve at their maximum level. Not having this extra time could explain why the children of the same intelligence who learned to read in school never caught up.

Since the IQ's of the children in the New York study were higher than in the California study (a range of 99 to 170 compared with 91 to 161), the results for the child of lower intelligence are less meaningful to us. But even in this group, over the three years, the effect of a head start in reading was greater for the ten children who had the lowest IQ's (between 99 and 124).

What does this mean to you?

What does all this tell us? Again, it's the home that makes the difference. The attitudes and values of the parent create the home environment that determines whether the child will have the greatest success in school. And knowing how to read guarantees success. Let's look at the data again.

All the children—those who read before school and those who didn't—had similar personality strengths. They had good memories; they were curious and persistent. They had similar intelligence. They came from similar educational and economic family backgrounds.

The difference was in their parents' attitudes. One-third of the parents of the non-early readers reported that their children had shown an interest in reading before school. But they gave them no help. Why?

As I mentioned before, one of the main reasons for not encouraging this interest was that the parents felt they would be interfering with the methods of the school. Parents have been made to feel that academic learning occurs only in school and that we shouldn't be involved in the process. Yet this doesn't make much sense. We see our children making all kinds of gains in every area of their lives outside school and don't hesitate to give every assistance we can.

We watch their physical progress with pleasure. They grow bigger and stronger. Their coordination becomes better. They can ride a bike, catch a ball, skip, hop, and jump a rope.

More important to school success, we notice their language development. They begin with one-word utterances and increase their vocabularies to thousands of words by the time they start kindergarten. Their sentences change from simple to complex. They become able to express their needs and feelings in words.

But we feel we should help them with their growth up to a point and then turn them over to the schools for "finishing." Why do we think that the six hours they're in school will have a greater effect than the time they spend outside of school? Much of the school day is involved with maintaining order, taking lunch and bathroom breaks, and shifting from one activity to another. The time spent in actual skill development is very little. The teacher—the most important factor in the classroom—must divide his or her time between 20 to 30 children. Yet we tend to leave the whole job of academic learning to the school.

It's in the home that you can give your child time to learn without pressure. (The teacher must chart progress in the classroom.) You can give him a variety of experiences. You can permit him to learn at his own rate—to explore and practice the skills he needs. (The teacher must use the methods of the school system.) You can give individual help by answering his particular questions about spelling and words. (The teacher must make general statements to cover the needs of all.) Only you can offer the one-to-one teaching relationship that is needed for the unique growth of your child.

In Durkin's study, many of the mothers who didn't help their children said they were "too busy." In most cases, they didn't work or have actual demands on them that occupied them so completely that they couldn't answer their child's questions. It was their attitude about helping that kept them from responding to their child's interest in spelling and words. Some said they had more than one child and didn't want to have to teach all of their children. One mother said she quickly discouraged an interest in printing because her child wanted to write all the time and had even written on the wall.

In contrast, the mothers who noted their child's early interest in printing and words verbalized their feelings of pleasure in teaching their child. They liked to spend time with him and watch him grow and change. They found his questions interesting; they responded with enthusiasm to his curiosity. One mother of an early reader said, "Gee, I enjoyed that child."

And most of these mothers never thought they were teaching. They felt they were just answering their child's questions, interacting with him, responding to his needs.

But what about the parents in the studies who did more—the ones who decided to go ahead and teach their child rather than wait for him to ask for help? Dr. Durkin thinks the child's own interest is important to make learning a pleasurable experience, and I agree.

But I think we create an interest in children when we read to them; when we surround them with alphabet blocks and stencils; when we provide them with alphabet books and word games. We don't reinforce that interest when we give them mechanical toys, motorized cars and trucks, and electronic gadgets. We must instill in them in the home that academic learning leads to success and happiness in life. We must introduce them to the pleasures of learning.

In short, I think that as parents we have to consciously decide what's important for our children. What do we really want for them? At Northwestern University, prospective teachers are advised to evaluate their lesson plans by asking, "What am I really teaching?" Parents are their child's most constant teachers and should ask themselves the same question.

Clearly, the parents of the early readers in Durkin's studies felt reading to be a valuable skill, and their home lives reflected that attitude. When they spent time and answered their child's questions, they began to lay the foundation for reading. When they read to him, they created in him a desire to learn to read while they taught him the language of books. When they provided writing materials and gave help with printing, they took the next step in the process toward mastery of the set of skills that constitutes reading.

You can do the same for your child. In fact, even if he's not a preschooler—if he's already a beginning reader or an upper elementary student—you can structure your home to encourage him to read. I'll give you specific instructions for each age group in chapters

5 through 9. But first, I want you to see how children learn at different ages so you'll understand the reasons for the instructions I give.

Chapter 4

Why you need to know about Piaget and Montessori

Let's take a minute to review what we've found out so far. First, a child's home environment is the most important factor for his success in school, and reading is the most important skill he can have. Second, as a parent, you can and should help your child learn pre-reading skills before he starts school and check on his progress as he goes through school to make sure he's learning to read well.

As your child's first teacher, you want to know how to be his best teacher. In this chapter, then, we'll see how your child begins to think and reason so that later on he can master the specific skills he needs to be able to read. For when you understand how he learns, you'll know how to present material to him in ways that will enable him to learn as easily as the children did in Dr. Durkin's studies.

To find out about a child's intellectual development, we'll look at the work of a Swiss psychologist, Jean Piaget, and an Italian doctor who became a schoolteacher, Maria Montessori. Though the results of their work show most strongly today in preschool education, you'll find their theories and research affect the way we teach children at any age.

How children learn

As a young man, Jean Piaget worked with the Binet Laboratory in Paris to standardize intelligence tests. On an intelligence test, there is only one right answer. But Piaget analyzed children's wrong answers to questions and noted two significant facts. First, many children gave the same wrong answers. Second, at different ages, the wrong answers they gave were the same. This suggested to Piaget that younger children think differently than older children. He wanted to discover how children think at different ages.

Since 1927, Piaget has observed, interviewed, and tested children of all ages to find out how intelligence develops. He has collected research from children in schools and in his laboratory in Geneva, Switzerland. But it was when he studied his own infants' behaviors that he gained his most conclusive insights into how children learn.

When Piaget watched his own three children in their cribs, he could see they were thinking even though they couldn't talk. As they interacted with their surroundings, he saw that they changed and adapted to solve problems.

You've probably noticed the same thing yourself. For example, when a child grasps a rattle for the first time, he doesn't know how to hold it. He drops it. After he tries again and again, he can coordinate his eyes and his hand to reach for it, to hold onto it with his fingers, and even to shake it to make a noise. The changes that occur in his approach and response to the problem are the result of his continued attempts to solve it.

As a result of his observations, Piaget views intelligence as the efficient processing of information. He sees intellectual development as a continual process of organization and reorganization. The child always builds on existing mental structures, using the knowledge he already has to try to solve each new problem. When the old methods don't work, he changes and adjusts them until they do work. In this way, he's always advancing his skills and changing his ideas about his world.

What causes him to continually experiment with new objects and behaviors? Curiosity is one of the key forces. When a child looks at a new object, curiosity prompts him to explore it using the behaviors he's already developed ... and to change those behaviors if they don't work. For example, when he first comes in contact with a ball, he tries to grasp it with the same movements that he uses to hold a rattle. When he can't pick it up with the same method, he changes his grasp.

Imitation also plays an important role in the child's development, says Piaget. From early infancy, the child watches others and tries to do what they do. If he hears a sound, he tries to reproduce that sound. If he sees a hand movement, he tries to make the same movement. In short, imitation and curiosity are two strong incentives in the learning process.

Piaget thinks that the child goes through four distinct stages in his intellectual growth. While he's in one of these periods, he's unable to see some of the obvious truths that in a later period, he can grasp easily. The order of these stages doesn't vary, and a child can't skip a stage entirely. Each stage lays the groundwork for the one that follows.

If we know what happens to the child in each of these stages, we know what kind of behavior to expect from him. We'll be able to understand why he acts the way he does. We'll be able to see his movement from one stage to the other. We'll be able to create an environment in the home that will meet his needs—that won't frustrate or hinder his progress.

The four stages of intellectual growth

A baby from birth to two years is in Piaget's sensori-motor stage. At this level, he thinks without language and learns primarily by touching, tasting, and doing. He uses the reflexes of sucking, crying, grasping, and flexing to interact with his environment. As he explores his world, these reflexes change into new structures.

For example, initially the baby only sucks the nipple or perhaps a finger that accidentally comes in contact with his mouth. Then he modifies his behavior to intentionally put his finger into his mouth. Later, he sucks on new objects like his blanket or toys to get information about them. So the sucking reflex is changed by the infant's experiences into a new structure that he can use to formulate ideas about his world.

In this period, Piaget says that the child has no object concept. He only sees pictures or images that come and go. If he can't see an object, he thinks it doesn't exist. He doesn't look for it. For example, if he sees his mother's face above his crib, he stares at it. When it disappears, he goes on to another activity.

But as he develops his thought process, he's able to formulate a mental picture and to remember it. That's why as he nears the end of this stage, he loves to play peek-a-boo and cries when his mother leaves the room.

This brings us to the pre-operational period, from two to seven years, when the child develops symbolic thought. Now, he can remember what has happened before and use that memory in new situations. For example, if he sees a pillow or blanket that reminds him of one of his own, he will playfully lie down, close his eyes, and pretend that he's going to sleep. To Piaget, this shows that child's play involves significant mental activity.

In this period, too, language changes in the same ways that the reflexes did in the sensori-motor stage. Now that the child can remember a mental picture of an object, he can use words to stand for things. For example, if you say "bicycle" to him, the word represents the object for him. He doesn't need to see the object to know what you mean.

With language, then, he labels objects and begins to classify them. The words take on broader meanings as he handles objects and forms ideas about them. His investigations reach a new level because he can use symbols in his thinking.

However, his concepts are really pre-concepts and his reasoning may be faulty. For example, the small child thinks that the tall, thin glass holds more water than the short, fat glass:

He thinks five pennies spread out are more than five pennies placed close together:

In other words, he can see only one aspect of a problem. He sees only the shape of the container and not the amount of liquid in it. He sees only the mass of pennies and not the number of pennies.

He classifies objects illogically. He can't put like things together. For example, in the beginning of this stage, he puts red and blue triangles and squares together. Later, he'll divide them into red and blue or squares and triangles.

As he explores his environment, he tests his ideas and conclusions. As always, he starts by using what he already knows and then modifies those ideas and methods when necessary as he adds to his knowledge of his world. Piaget says that if the child doesn't do this testing, he won't be able to think logically.

Piaget's observations in the pre-operational period have had a great impact on nursery schools. Because educators know that children learn from a variety of experiences, they've changed their teacher-directed learning programs to activity centers so the child can do his own experiments and draw his own conclusions.

To illustrate, let's take a look at a typical nursery school today:

A little boy is painting at an easel. He starts with a small dot of red paint and then makes dots all over the paper. Finally, he joins all the dots and covers his entire paper with red paint. His teacher asks him if he has finished, tells him he did a good job, and hangs his painting up to dry.

At the sandbox, three children fill and empty assorted cups, funnels, and containers. At the water tables, one child washes a doll and the other, a set of miniature dishes. The children are completely absorbed in these activities and only receive occasional comments from a teacher to "keep the sand in the sandbox and the water in the dishpans."

In the block corner, four children build various structures. They don't build together; each makes his own creation. They construct a garage, a tower, a roadway, a train track.

In the housekeeping corner, one child puts a "baby" to rest, rocks the crib, and sings to it. Another "washes" the dishes, while the third child mops the floor vigorously. Every day they come to school and go through the same play routine.

At several tables throughout the room, children put puzzles together, draw with stencils, string beads, count sticks, or match geometric blocks to cards that have the same shapes drawn on them. At another large table, a teacher helps children do an art project.

What do the children learn from these activities? As the little boy paints at the easel, he expands his ideas about colors. As the children empty and fill containers with sand and water, they learn about the characteristics of those materials, and they discover that the amount of the material doesn't necessarily change with the size and shape of the container. When they build with blocks, they see part-to-whole relationships. In the housekeeping corner, they learn language and imitate adults. As they examine the different size and shape manipulatives (puzzle pieces, beads, geometric blocks, etc.), they develop number, color, and shape concepts. These enable them to sort and classify the objects in their environment. According to Piaget, all of these skills are needed for the next level of development.

From age seven to eleven years, the child moves to the concrete operations stage. In this period, the child organizes his environment with no conflicts in his thought process. Now he puts it all together. Reasoning results from his previous explorations.

In this stage, the child can sort objects by their properties and classify them into ranking orders. For example, from his experiences he concludes that all cats have fur and whiskers and say "meow." He observes that all dogs have fur, bark, and wag their tails. He understands that the term *animals* includes dogs and cats.

He has concepts of large and small, long and short, and thick and thin. He knows the difference between sand and water, a solid and a liquid. He can differentiate between colors and shapes. He recognizes the categories of soft and hard, rough and smooth, light and heavy.

Now he can place objects in order from the shortest to the tallest when before he placed them randomly and illogically:

pre-operational   concrete operations

In the earlier stage, he could only focus on one characteristic—putting them in order. He couldn't pay attention to the length of the sticks at the same time.

Now he can solve problems of one-to-one correspondence. Without counting, he can correctly pair the flowers to the vases shown below. When he was younger, he would put the flowers close together in a row opposite the vases:

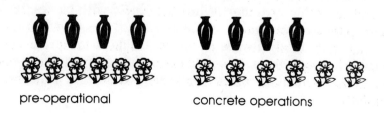

pre-operational   concrete operations

Now he can understand conservation of material. For example, in the pre-operational stage when he was younger, if he were shown two balls of clay, he would say they contained the same amount of material. But if the shape of one ball were changed to a sausage, he would say the sausage had more clay in it:

In contrast, in the concrete operations stage, the child can focus on several aspects of a problem at the same time. He can attend to changes. So he can see that when he changes the shape of the clay, he doesn't change the amount.

Now the child can think in abstract terms in what Piaget calls logico-mathematical thinking. In my first-grade class, I had the children add two sets of two poker chips. Then I said, "Well, you can do this to add things together. Or you can draw it like this:"

"Or ..." and a boy called out, "You can do it really fast and write 2 + 2 = 4."

These are the kinds of abstractions a child must be able to make before he can read. He must know that he can say the word *boy*, draw a picture of a boy, or write *boy* and mean the same thing. Piaget believes that unless the child has had enough experiences with actual objects, he won't be able to make such transfers.

The final stage of development is formal operations from eleven years old to adult. Now the child can form hypotheses without handling objects. He considers what events would occur under possible conditions. He can make inferences, draw conclusions, and think abstractly on the highest level. He can use logical thinking to do algebra and to conduct scientific experiments. He can use reading in all the content areas to solve problems with creativity.

How does a child move from one level of development to another?

A child doesn't automatically move from one stage to another as he grows older. Instead, Piaget sees several forces that cause the child to change his thinking.

First, as the child grows and develops, his physical capacity increases, and he must have this maturation to change his thinking. The smaller and lighter brain of the newborn cannot learn as much as that of the older child. Before his vocal apparatus develops, the child cannot speak. Before his muscles strengthen, he cannot walk.

Social forces also affect the intellectual growth of the child. When he talks with his parents, does his own reading, goes to school, mingles with his peers, imitates others, he learns.

But the basic force at work, as I've already indicated several times, is the child's own experimentation and interaction with his environment. Piaget believes that contact with objects results in changes in perceptions. Before the child can classify objects, he must see some of them. Before he can speak, he must hear people talk. In order to think logically and learn concepts, he must form an idea about an object or situation and then modify that idea when he discovers another feature that he didn't see before.

For example, as we saw earlier, when a child in the preoperational stage sees water in two different containers, he can only focus on the shape of the glasses. He sees that one is tall and thin; the other, short and fat. He thinks the taller one holds more water. When he pours the liquid himself from a measuring cup and finds that the amount of water is the same in both containers, he's presented with a contradiction. To make sense out of these two facts, he changes his previous ideas. He moves to a new level of thinking.

Piaget concludes that the ways an individual adapts and organizes his thinking depend on his environment and his learning history. For example, one of Piaget's children was born in the winter and spent the early months of her life bundled in warm clothes that confined her movements. When he compared her development with that of his other children at the same age, he noted that her hand-eye coordination had been restricted. If the child's world offers limited opportunity for exploration, his growth will reflect those limitations.

Development, then, is a gradual and continuous process. But it depends on the environment and the ways that the child acts upon it. If the child doesn't have the right experiences, he won't learn to his fullest.

What kind of an environment will provide optimum growth? Maria Montessori has the answer.

"The prepared environment"

As part of her advanced medical training, Maria Montessori was assigned to the psychiatric clinic in Rome for "mentally defective" children. To treat these children, she taught them. Her methods were so successful that her students passed the state tests for primary certificates. If she could obtain such results with mentally retarded children, what could she do with normal children?

Maria Montessori studied at the University of Rome and observed children in schools before she established her famous Children's House in the slums of Rome in 1907. From her observations of children and her theories of learning, she developed the methods and materials that have had an impact on education since their first appearance. We can easily see the similarities between Montessori and Piaget as we study her work.

Like Piaget, Montessori believed that the child's education begins at birth. She thought the most important years for learning are from birth to age six. Her methods come from her observation that the naturally curious child teaches himself as he explores his environment. She saw education as a step-by-step progression with each advance based on previous experiences.

Her school became a "prepared environment," a well-planned, structured setting for learning. Within this orderly arrangement, the child can choose his own activities. However, all the exercises and games lead him to a mastery of reading, writing, and arithmetic. In short, Montessori organized the classroom so the child can only choose from activities with educational goals.

This doesn't mean that each activity teaches mastery of a specific subject. Instead, they teach more general skills that help the child have success in many different areas. The child does the same activities again and again until the movements and procedures are a part of his natural behavior. Then, he uses these patterns in his next level of development.

Montessori's curriculum stresses development in three areas—motor activity (movement and coordination), sensory perceptions, and language. This reflects her ideas about how and what young children learn. She believed that in the first six years the child develops the large and small muscle coordination that stays with him all his life. She thought his interaction with objects in his environment should build this coordination while it stimulates his senses of sight, hearing, and touch. She also felt that language and sensory education are closely connected. Words label perceptions—*soft, hard, long, short,* etc.—and experiences give meaning to the words.

Montessori felt that children should be free to move as they learn, so she designed the environment to permit the child's natural movements. She removed the stationary desks of the traditional classroom and replaced them with child-sized tables and chairs. She also provided little pieces of carpet so the child could put his work on the floor and have his own space.

She used normal, daily domestic tasks to help the child build graceful body movements and improve his coordination. For example, when the child sets the table, washes the floor, or shines shoes in a Montessori classroom, he practices the movements that train his body to do other activities. At the same time, he learns a step-by-step order for everyday routines.

Other Montessori learning activities are designed to develop the child's small muscle coordination. When the child buttons, hooks, laces, or ties pieces of cloth together, he learns the skills he needs to dress himself. When he uses geometric shape stencils to produce designs, he strengthens his finger muscles and learns the outlines of the basic shapes so that later on, he can print the letters of the alphabet.

The emphasis on geometric shapes is also found in many of the activities Montessori developed to teach visual awareness. In one activity, the child orders circles from smallest to largest. In another, he fits different-sized cylinders into a board with matching different-sized holes. In a third, he works with geometric insets of various sizes and shapes, matching each wooden shape to the space that it fits in a frame. As he does these exercises, he develops his senses of sight and touch more fully until he can recognize a variety of sizes and shapes—a skill that prepares him to recognize the letters of the alphabet.

To increase auditory perception, the child works with "sound boxes." These little wooden boxes are filled with different materials, such as sand, gravel, flaxseed, and stones ... two boxes each with the same material. The child listens to the sound of a box. Then, he shakes the other boxes to find the one that has the same sound. In this way, he learns to "hear" different sounds—a skill that prepares him to tell the differences between the sounds of the letters.

To improve the sense of touch, one activity requires a child to be blindfolded. He then matches pieces of cloth of different textures—velvets, wools, cottons, etc.—by feeling them. In this way, he learns the meaning of *smooth, silky, coarse,* and *fine.* Exercises with letters cut out of sandpaper also refine his sense of touch as they teach him the alphabet.

To Montessori, teachers are facilitators, helpers to the child, supplying him with language to describe his world. They help him learn when they show him by their own actions how to do a task. They teach him language when they speak clearly and meaningfully. The child's own interest and curiosity cause him to watch, listen to, and imitate his teachers.

As the child explores his environment, teachers observe his progress. When they see that he has mastered a task, they add the language he needs for his thought development. For example, they give him labels for the objects he handles in the classroom. Or they merely point to the object and say, "This is red" or "This is blue." They always use few words to avoid confusing the child. They are models for language.

How Piaget and Montessori changed the classroom

As I said earlier, Piaget's conclusions that children need many experiences before they can master concepts and skills changed the curriculum of the schools, particularly of nursery schools. Discovery learning became the design of the classroom. Interest centers—the block corner, housekeeping corner, art table, puzzle center, sand and water tables, math activity area, etc.—replaced traditional teacher-directed programs.

Maria Montessori's creative exercises that teach skills and concepts became part of these interest centers. Her lacing and buttoning frames, sound boxes, graduated cylinders, geometric shape activities, and sandpaper letters are standard childhood equipment. Her concept of child-directed learning dominates early childhood education.

Piaget and Montessori have shown teachers that the child doesn't learn when he listens to the teacher tell him about his world. He learns when he examines objects in his environment and has experiences that illustrate ideas.

For example, he doesn't learn what a square is when he sees a picture of one. He develops a concept of "squareness" when he stacks square blocks, traces with square stencils, matches a square shape to a square pattern on a board, works at a square table, sits on a square rug.

He learns words when they are part of his daily life—when they have meaning in his existence. For example, if he arranges sticks in order from shortest to tallest, he learns the meaning of *short* and *tall*. If he orders color samples from lightest to darkest, he learns the meaning of *light* and *dark*. If he puts cylinders in a board from smallest to largest, he understands *small* and *large*.

As a result, many teachers today try to find ways for the child to see for himself—to figure out his own way to do tasks—and they arrange their classrooms accordingly. They select activities that teach specific skills. They choose exercises that the child can do by himself to teach himself. They set up experiments so the child can draw conclusions from his own efforts.

They give him language to label his world. They provide the words that describe what he sees, hears, and feels. They require that he say these words to practice his understanding of them. They stimulate his curiosity to use his knowledge every day and add to it.

They take him on field trips—to the supermarket, firehouse, police station, hospital. They take him to the circus, plays, puppet shows, pantomimes. They take him to the historical and natural history museums, the aquarium, and the planetarium. They try to give him real-life experiences that show him what words mean.

What does this mean to you?

Your home can be a "prepared environment." You can plan what you want your child to learn and create a setting that will teach him the skills he needs for success in school. You can give him the atmosphere that urges him to explore and experiment. You can choose activities that are right for his level of development, that will challenge him without frustrating him.

You can use the daily activities of your home to develop your child's large and small muscles as well as his language and thinking. When he helps you wash the floor, sweep the sidewalk, plant in the garden, or shovel the snow, he learns about the properties of objects and materials. He sees how water changes from clear to cloudy, how a broom works to clean the walk, how seeds turn into flowers, how snow piles up when you move it from here to there.

You can develop his language in your home when you talk and read to him every day. You can be the model for the speech that he imitates. You can give him the words for the objects and materials he sees.

When you take him with you on your errands every day, you can use these experiences to teach him new words and expand his ideas about his world. You can pull out the important information from the vast confusion of stimuli. You can help him understand the concepts he needs to build on.

As his teacher, you can direct his learning to reading, writing, and arithmetic. You can choose activities that develop his senses of sight, hearing, and touch to prepare him to recognize his letters and the sounds they represent. You can give him the time to repeat activities so that he masters the movements and concepts he needs to be able to advance in his skills. You can prepare him for success in school.

Chapter 5

How I raised the IQ's of 10 "unteachable" children

The children in my language group were five years old. Yet they didn't know the names of the colors. They couldn't count. They'd never heard of a square, a rectangle, or a triangle.

They didn't have words to label and order their worlds. For example, they were familiar with *big* and *little* but didn't understand *large* and *small*. They used gestures and cried to communicate their needs and feelings.

Every object was a "thing." They waved their hands about to describe these "things." They couldn't relate an incident that happened at home or on the way to school. They didn't know how to say that they were tired or hungry. They couldn't tell me when someone hurt them.

The 200 children in the open classroom* of my school came to kindergarten with a wide range of skills. Some spoke fluently, knew their colors, shapes, sizes, numbers, and letters, and had begun to read. Most knew some of these concepts and showed interest in the alphabet and books, though they didn't have enough skills to read yet. But the ten children in my language group couldn't even talk well enough to express their basic needs.

---

*My school was made up of huge classrooms of open space that could be divided into smaller areas with low storage units. The kindergarten classroom, or "pod," had 200 children, 12 teachers, and four aides in an 8,000 square-foot area.

The Peabody Picture Vocabulary Test

At the start of school, the team of 12 teachers in the pod tested all the children on the Peabody Picture Vocabulary Test to find out how much language they understood. This test measures receptive language. These aren't necessarily the words that the child uses in his speech, but they're words that he knows the meaning of when someone else says them. To show his understanding on the test, the child doesn't have to say the word. He must point to the picture on the page that depicts the word the tester says.

The test begins with words for common objects in the environment, such as *table, chair, horse,* etc. It gets progressively more complex as it asks the child to recognize words of action, such as *sitting* and *teaching.* Then, it shows words of classification, such as *transportation* and *communication.* The 150 items in the test represent the vocabulary that is normal for each age from two to eighteen years.

The Peabody Picture Vocabulary Test can also be used as a measure of intelligence. Intelligence tests evaluate what a child has learned by comparison with what other children know at the same age. Before a child reads, a language test is one of the ways to measure what he knows. If a child has a large vocabulary, it shows that he's had many experiences and that he understands those experiences. With language he tells others how much knowledge he's acquired.

To find the child's intelligence quotient (IQ), you compare the mental age derived from a test with the child's actual chronological age. For example, if the child's score on the Peabody Picture Vocabulary Test is 2.5 (meaning he understands words of an average two-and-one-half-year-old child) and his actual age is five years, his intelligence quotient is 50:

$$\frac{2.5 \text{ (mental age)}}{5 \text{ (chronological age)}} \times 100 = 50 \text{ (intelligence quotient)}$$

The "average" range of intelligence is from 90 to 110. One child in six has an intelligence quotient of less than 85. You can see that an IQ of 50 indicates a level far below average.

The children

Half of the children in my language group didn't even get the number of right answers that's expected of an average two-and-one-half-year-old. Since they were almost five years old, their scores on the Peabody translated to IQ's of 50 or below, as in the example above. By school standards, these children were "unteachable." Some of them had already been recommended for an evaluation for learning handicaps. But since they were so young, the staff hoped that these learning difficulties would go away as the children had more experiences in a stimulating environment.

The ten children represented many different cultures and ethnic backgrounds. Four were white, four were black, one was American Indian, and one was Hispanic. There were two girls and eight boys (traditionally, more boys than girls have learning disabilities). Their parents' jobs ranged from professions that require a college education to janitorial services.

But the children all shared the problem of neglect in the home. No one had ever listened or talked to any of them. One child was the youngest in a wealthy family where the mother frequently took trips. Only two of the children in the group had a father in the home. Three were in the custody of a legal guardian instead of a natural parent.

This neglect was especially obvious in their lack of language. They'd never learned the labels that they had to know to be able to tell others about what they'd seen or what they needed.

But their need showed in other ways too. They'd never learned how to listen or follow directions or pay attention to details. They'd never learned to memorize or concentrate or wait for their turn. They had very short attention spans. They were highly distractible. They cried and called out at any time. They squirmed and wriggled.

In fact, none of these children could sit still for more than a few minutes. They reached out to touch specks of dirt or lint on the floor. They became preoccupied with tying and untying their shoelaces. They became involved with their neighbor's clothing or hair. They were disturbed if someone bumped them accidentally or moved into their space on the floor.

When I took them anywhere in a group, they never lined up in an orderly procession. One always held my hand and jumped up and down beside me. The rest straggled behind. They pulled on each other, sucked their fingers, grabbed at objects, bumped into the furniture and walls, tripped and fell down as we went along. They cried out when they hurt themselves or saw something that attracted their attention.

My plan

I was determined to bridge the gap for them. I knew that if I taught them words for common objects, they would be able to use those words in their daily lives. I expected that if I read books to them, they would learn to understand school vocabulary and sentence structure. I anticipated that if I gave them many experiences planned to teach specific skills, they would master the notions of color, size, shape, and texture that they needed to begin to read.

I loved each one of them, and they knew it because I smiled a lot and touched them gently. One of them always held my hand during class and another patted my leg. They wanted to feel the physical comfort of the warmth of another human being who cared.

I only spoke to them in a quiet voice and tried to appear very calm and relaxed. I knew they had a lot of tension in their homes. When I acted calm, they relaxed. They trusted me to lead them.

I gave them only positive feedback. They had already decided that they couldn't do things. I had to show them that they could. Often, I said to them, "Good, that's good."

I never scolded them when they made mistakes. I ignored all their "bad" behavior. If I said, "Oh, I love the way Mike is sitting and John is sitting," etc., the rest sat right down and waited for me to say the same thing about them. When I called attention to their "good" behavior, I helped them to learn new, school-appropriate ways to act.

The activities I used in the classroom

Team teaching in an open classroom makes it possible to divide children into groups by their skill levels. After giving several tests to evaluate the children in the pod, we teachers held small language groups every day for an hour and a half so we could meet the special needs of each group.

Each time I met with my ten children I followed the same schedule. Their behaviors reflected the confusion of their homes. They needed a regular routine to give them security. Throughout the language period, they would get agitated and ask, "What are we going to do next?" A regular routine let them know that every day would be the same. They could then relax and pay attention because they knew from their own experience what to expect.

A story

I began every language period by seating them in front of me on the floor. To get their attention, I read them a story that had a simple plot and pictures clearly associated with the words. Even though none of them were bilingual, they hadn't been exposed to good language patterns. Consequently, they couldn't attend to a story unless they could easily see the connection between the words and the actions of the story. Line drawings composed of only one object on a page made this connection for them.

In the beginning of the year, I had trouble holding their attention because nothing I read had much meaning for them in their previous experience. Animal stories had the greatest appeal. *Are You My Mother?* by P. D. Eastman was their favorite. It's an uncomplicated story about a bird who can't find his mother after he comes out of the egg. They identified with the fright of the baby bird whose mother is missing and who doesn't know what she looks like. The pictures clearly depict the words of the story (see figure 5-1), and the children always became very absorbed and sat very quietly. The story taught them the meanings of words and the sentence structure of standard English.

The children also related well to *The Best Nest*, *I Wish That I Had Duck Feet*, and *Put Me in the Zoo*. These Dr. Seuss Beginner Books all appealed to them because of the content, the simple sentence structure, and the great amount of repetition.

I read their favorite stories week after week. It wasn't long before all of them sat down quietly the minute they saw me reach for a book. Now they paid attention because they understood what I read. As their vocabularies increased and their sentence patterns became firmly established, I read longer and more involved books.

A change of pace

After the story, we played "Follow the Leader." I knew they couldn't sit still for long and needed to move about to release their tension.

Down, out of the tree
he went.

16

Figure 5-1 A page from *Are You My Mother?*

Very quietly, with no words at all, I put my hands on my head, on my shoulders, on my knees, and back to my head, on my waist, behind my back. They needed to watch me to be able to do what I did. This taught them to pay close attention to me at all times.

Memory training

To communicate with others, a child must remember words and be able to recall them at the appropriate time. But if no one ever listens to him, he doesn't develop these skills.

That was the case with the children in my language group. So now I began to train their memories. With a calendar, I said the days of the week with them, pointing to each day as I said it. Then, each child took a turn and recited the days in order on his own. I simply listened, giving the children a chance to practice the words and helping them as needed. When each could finally do this alone, I gave a baseball card as a prize.

This was the first step. Always, the child builds on a foundation of knowledge. After he learns the days of the week, he adds the order and the names of the months of the year. Slowly, he develops a general understanding of time, a notion of the rhythm and the regularity of nature. Day follows night; months are made of days; years are made of months.

Later in the school year, after they learned the days of the week, we recited nursery rhymes together. Mother Goose held their attention and taught them new words.

Labels for objects

Next, I showed the children a set of pictures from the Peabody Language Kit. These are very simple, colorful representations of all classifications of items in the environment. There are birds, animals, shapes, numbers, fruits, vegetables, objects in the home, vehicles, and people. My goal was to increase their vocabularies by showing them pictures that clearly depicted the words that I taught them. I hoped that later on when they heard a word, they would recall a specific image.

I began with pictures of animals because the children were interested in them. In the early part of the year, though, the animals all looked alike to them. To be able to attach a name to an animal, they had to learn to notice the differences between all of them. Thus, these pictures trained them to pay attention to details.

For example, in the beginning of this language drill, they couldn't tell the difference between a wolf and a fox, a skunk and a porcupine, a horse and a donkey. Later, they had the same difficulty with other categories. With fruits and vegetables, they confused cabbage and lettuce, strawberries and cherries. With objects around the home, they continually mixed up a mop and a broom, a rake and a shovel, a table and a desk.

I helped them to differentiate when I pointed out the distinct differences. A skunk has a white stripe and gives off a bad smell. A porcupine has sharp quills which hurt. Cherries are round. Strawberries have a different, more pointed shape and little spots on them.

In this way, I drew their attention to the special characteristics of each object. I always clearly explained my words. As I spoke, I put my finger on the white stripe of the skunk and on the sharp quills of the porcupine. I drew my finger around the outline of the cherry and the pointed shape of the strawberry. I touched the spots of the strawberry with short, light taps of my finger.

To teach them, I said, "The name of this animal is *skunk*. Now you say it." And every child said with me, "*skunk*." I repeated the same basic sentence throughout the lesson.

As the days went by, I held up a picture, called on a specific child, and asked, "What is the name of this animal?" And each child had to recall the correct word that identified the picture.

Later, the pictures were simple outlines of actions, such as raking leaves, hoeing the garden, sweeping the floor, climbing the stairs, or washing the windows. I made them give me the phrases. When they could, I praised them and smiled. When they couldn't, I helped them and supplied the words they lacked.

Games

After 15 minutes of this intense direct language drill, I changed the pace to a game that was designed to teach a specific skill. We know that learning becomes integrated into the child's mental structures when he uses his knowledge in his environment. When he listens to language and then performs a behavior, he proves that he understands. Games give opportunities for children to listen to directions and then carry out the commands.

To give them a chance to use the new words and sentence patterns they were acquiring, I made a lotto game. From two identical alphabet workbooks from the variety store, I cut out pictures that represented ten different categories of common items: objects found in school; objects found in the bathroom; objects found in the living room; different occupations; kinds of transportation; articles of clothing; colors; shapes; animals; and fruits and vegetables.

I took ten pieces of cardboard and pasted eight different but related pictures on each one. (In other words, each piece of cardboard contained all the pictures for a single category.) The matching pictures I pasted on square index cards.

To play the game, each child got a board similar to the one in figure 5-2 (the transportation card). The small, matching cards were put facedown in the center of a circle of children. I would choose a card, hold it up, and say, "Who has the *school bus*?" The child with the transportation card would have to check his board and say, "I have the school bus," before he could get it. The "winner" was the child who completed his board first.

In this way, the children learned to look carefully at their boards, to remember what was on them, and to match the card that I held up to one on their boards. This game required that they pay attention, follow directions, wait for a turn, and speak in a loud, clear voice. It helped them to classify objects in their environment as it reinforced their language skills.

We also played an action game that taught them the names of the colors and their body parts. In this activity, I gave a command such as, "If you're wearing blue, stand up." "If you're wearing white, touch your elbows." "If you're wearing brown, put your thumbs on your wrists." I always showed them what I wanted to do. They were learning by doing.

A complete understanding, as Piaget and Montessori have shown us, is derived from many experiences in the environment. For example, as the child explores his world, he develops a general idea for *red*. It's the color of an apple, a shirt, a candy cane, a hair ribbon, jello. It's not always the same shade of red. Slowly, the child formulates a notion of *red*.

To teach the concept of color, one game we played was "Fish." From construction paper, I cut fish of the eight major colors—red, orange, blue, purple, green, yellow, black, and brown. I put a paper clip on each fish. The "fishing pole" was a string with a magnet tied to it. The "pond" was a dishpan. When they "caught" a fish, they had to tell me its color. Then, they could keep it until the game was over.

Figure 5-2 Lotto game board

For another color game, I made "lollipops" from circles cut from colored construction paper and glued onto wooden sticks. I went around the circle of children, and they chose from a selection of five different colors. If they could name the color, they could keep the "lollipop" until the game was over.

Many games that teach colors and shapes are possible with a selection of attribute blocks. Large and small, thick and thin triangles, rectangles, circles, squares, and hexagons that are just the right size for a kindergartner's hands compose a set. Mine had three colors—red, blue, and yellow. With these blocks, the child learns the distinctive features of each shape. When he holds them, he can see and feel the differences in their forms.

To play, we sat in a circle. Each child in my group chose a shape. He pointed to the shape he wanted and then named it. I gave them free time to experiment with these blocks. They arranged them in patterns, stacked them, and built with them.

After a few minutes, I gave them directions to follow. "Put the small, red blocks in the center of the circle." And everyone would put all their small, red shapes in the center. This called their attention to the color, *red*, and the size, *small*.

Then, I gave a new command. "Put your thin blocks in the center of the circle." And everyone had to think about the feature of *thinness*. Each new direction clearly illustrated a different attribute of color, texture, or shape.

For more practice in shape recognition, we played a game I made with aluminum pie plates. On each plate I pasted either a circle, a triangle, a square, or a rectangle cut from construction paper. I only used three colors for each shape—red, blue, and yellow.

We played this in the manner of a quiz show. I was the "master of ceremonies," the children, the "audience" for the child who had a turn. To play the game, I gave a direction to the child, such as "Pick up the blue triangle," and the child selected the correct pie plate from those in the center of the circle of children. When the child did it right, I acted surprised and enormously pleased.

To give them a chance to handle different materials and textures, I filled ten shoe boxes with various objects. To concentrate on naming these objects, I asked them to follow my directions and "take out the *pencil*"; then, the *cotton ball*, the *feather*, *spoon*, etc. To learn texture words, I asked them to take out a *soft* object, a *fluffy* object, etc. When they mastered these terms, to focus on the materials of each object, I asked them to take out the one made of *wood*, *metal*, *fur*, *cotton*, etc.

All the games increased the language skills of the children as they listened and followed directions. Their interest kept them motivated to pay attention and to wait for their turn. They quickly learned the names for the colors and shapes and textures as they used these materials every day.

Paper and pencil tasks

Their small muscle coordination, however, was poor. They didn't hold pencils properly. They couldn't draw anything. Part of the problem was that they hadn't had opportunities to practice. But they also had poor self-concepts. Each one would cry out, "I can't do it," before he even tried.

To prepare them to write and to teach them shapes, I made my own clay dough. I gave each one a ball of clay. Together we rolled the balls into sausages and then patted them back into balls again. We shaped them into triangles and then into squares. We experimented with changes in the form of the clay.

On other days, I gave each one a ball of clay and a different cookie cutter. I had squares, diamonds, stars, hearts, and circles for them to cut out. With these activities, they strengthened their finger muscles and learned new words as they explored a new material.

For another activity that taught small muscle coordination, I took ten plastic meat trays from the supermarket and filled them with sand. Using these, they drew the shapes with their fingers in the sand as you do at the beach. This helped them develop a feeling for the shape they would later draw with a writing instrument.

With pencils, they traced the insides of large metal stencils of different geometric shapes. Then they colored in the shape that resulted. At first, they cried out in frustration when they tried to color within the outline of the shapes they made. As the days went by, their coordination improved. They became pleased with their efforts and wanted to do this activity again and again.

I gave each child a 9 x 12-inch chalkboard. Together we drew a circle, a triangle, a square, and a rectangle. Since they had become familiar with the shapes using clay, sand, and stencils, they made these forms with chalk easily.

After they could draw these basic shapes, every day I gave them a simple outline to color with crayons. In the beginning of the year, the drawings were of animals because they learned the names of animals in their daily language drills. Then, they did vegetables, fruits, etc. (See figures 5-3 and 5-4.)

Cow

Figure 5-3 Cow coloring sheet

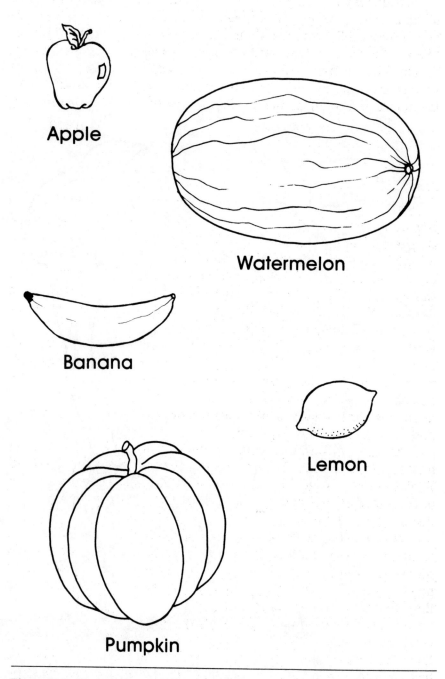

Figure 5-4 Fruits coloring sheet

After they had learned their colors and the names for all these objects, they advanced to Mother Goose rhyme pictures, like the one in figure 5-5. I directed them to color these in specific ways. For "Peter, Peter, Pumpkin Eater," the instructions were as follows: "Make Peter's hair yellow; make the pumpkin orange; make his wife's dress blue;" etc. This strengthened their understanding of the colors and required them to listen carefully to follow directions.

Art

Art activities also gave them opportunities to work with colors, shapes, and textures and to improve their coordination. For example, we made pictures like the ones in figure 5-6 using pre-cut construction paper. As part of this activity, they learned to put paste on the shapes with only one finger. (This took all year to learn. For much of the year, they used all their fingers and put the paste everywhere.)

To make a texture collage, I cut shapes from different fabrics— white furry rectangles, yellow ribbed squares, red silky triangles, black velvet circles, blue striped rectangles, thick yellow yarn strands. They created their own two-dimensional pictures as they pasted the pieces on paper. They loved to feel the different materials. Art activities like these improved their visual, tactile, and small muscle development.

As their skills increased, we made books. Few of them had books in their homes. They needed to see how books are created. They needed to know they could do it themselves. They were proud of their own efforts and looked at the books again and again on the bus on the way home.

For example, we made a color book with each page having one of the pictures shown in figure 5-7. They cut out the pictures and pasted them in their own books with the correct color word on each page. It was difficult for them to cut, so I made the outlines large so they could all have success.

We also made several books with pictures cut from magazines. One had different kinds of transportation—boat, car, plane, and train. One was on sports—baseball, football, golf, tennis, basketball, boxing, and skiing. Another had farm animals—cat, dog, pig, cow, and horse.

29

PETER, PETER, PUMPKIN EATER

Peter, Peter, pumpkin eater,
Had a wife and couldn't keep her;
He put her in a pumpkin shell,
And there he kept her very well.

Figure 5-5 Peter, Peter, Pumpkin Eater coloring sheet

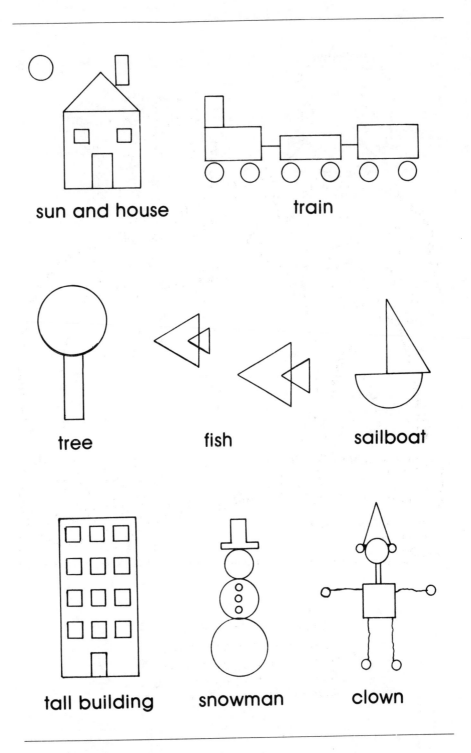

sun and house   train

tree   fish   sailboat

tall building   snowman   clown

Figure 5-6 Shape pictures

green

blue

red

yellow

purple

orange

brown

white

Figure 5-7 Color book

Other language aids

Sequence cards gave the children a chance to put events in order and to tell about them. The children had to arrange the pictures and then describe the action in each picture. For example, one group of cards I used shows a girl buying shoes at a store (see figure 5-8). The child must say that first, the girl goes to the store; second, the man measures her foot; third, she tries on the shoes and tells the man that she wants them; and last, she pays for them and leaves the store.

Other types of teaching cards are available, too. With one set, the child must name the picture and give its opposite. Examples are *day* and *night*, *up* and *down*, *in* and *out*, *light* and *dark*. With another set of cards, the child must tell what's missing in the picture or what's wrong. These activities require the child to look carefully and think. They help him learn words that order his environment.

Following directions

As their language became more elaborate, I gave the children more complicated directions to follow. I gave them words to describe what they did. When they followed my commands, they proved to me that they understood the meaning of the words they heard.

A board covered with flannel acts like a magnet. When you place flannel cutouts on it, they stick. The flannel board offered another opportunity for language use. I gave the children instructions similar to the following: "Put the red man in the middle of the board. Put the brown house next to him. Put two green trees on the other side of the man. Put a yellow sun in the sky."

The results

As the year went on, I saw a steady improvement in the children's skills, coordination, and desire to learn. They began to have success in their efforts with chalk and crayons. Now they wanted to do other writing. When they came to school in the morning, they went to the easel and painted squares and circles and triangles. Next, they drew houses from these shapes in the same way that we had made the shape pictures with construction paper. Later, they began to print the alphabet.

1. The girl goes to the shoe store.

2. The man measures her foot.

Figure 5-8   Sequence cards (part 1 of 2)

3. She tries on the shoes and tells the man she likes them.

4. The girl and her mother pay for the shoes and leave the store.

Figure 5-8 Sequence cards (part 2 of 2)

Now that they knew how to enjoy other pastimes, they began to act differently. Instead of hitting and running around the room when they came to school in the morning, they began to do puzzles and quiet activities. Sometimes they took one of my books and read. At first, in direct imitation of me, they held the book out to the side as I did when I read to the class. They copied me because they had never seen anyone read a book for pleasure.

Now the children could express their needs and wants clearly. Because I listened to them, they told me what happened at home, in the lunchroom, on the bus. They told me when they were hungry, didn't feel well, needed a Band-Aid.

In April, they were re-tested on the Peabody Picture Vocabulary Test. Every one of them had made significant gains. All had increased their scores by two or more years.

When these scores were translated into intelligence quotients, the increases were even more significant. The child who had scored 2.5 in September now tested at 4.5. His IQ had gone from 50 to 80:

$$\frac{4.5 \text{ (mental age)}}{5.6 \text{ (chronological age)}} \times 100 = \frac{450}{5.6} = 80 \text{ IQ}$$

There's no doubt that these children were slow learners. Educators refer to children with an IQ range of 75 to 90 as "dull normal" or "low average." Their mental age always lags behind their chronological age. In most cases, the slow learner never catches up to his peers.

But because of the progress they'd made, it was obvious these children *could* learn. So for every one of them that was re-tested, the examiner recommended a similarly stimulating learning environment in the future to maintain his gain and to close the gap between him and his peers.

At the end of the year, the children began to write the letters of the alphabet in the same way that early in the year they had learned the geometric shapes. When they could tell the difference between a triangle and a circle, they could also learn the details of an *A* and an *O*. When they could classify *red* and *blue* as colors, they could learn that *A* and *O* are letters of the alphabet. They passed all Chicago Level A kindergarten tests to determine reading readiness.

What does this mean to you?

These children lagged far behind their classmates in the skills they had mastered before they came to school. They needed direct instruction to close the gap. They needed a program designed to teach specific concepts—color, size, shape, and texture—and specific language—vocabulary and sentence structure.

They needed praise to give them confidence. They had to know that what they did was all right. They had to be told often that they could do it.

They needed many experiences to teach them about materials and objects. During the year, we went on many field trips as a class—to a farm, the zoo, the botanical garden, the aquarium. We saw the circus, a puppet show, a pantomime, a play. We went to the park and on short walks in the neighborhood. They had to see in real life the animals and the items that were in the pictures and books they saw every day in class.

They needed an opportunity to use the language they heard. When they played games and did art projects, they practiced the words that were in their books. When they sang songs and followed directions, they learned what the words meant.

They needed order and simplicity. The daily routine and the often-repeated activities provided the order. The direct focus of the games and exercises told them again and again what they needed to know. The class schedule was set up to say the same things in many different ways.

From this special classroom account, you can see how a child learns what he needs to know to have success in school. You can see how, as his teacher, you can create a learning environment that specifically guides your child to master the important ideas he needs to express himself clearly, to understand what others say, and to learn skills that prepare him to read.

From an hour and a half a day of direct instruction, five days a week, the children in my group increased their language to the level they needed to begin to read. They learned to notice the necessary details they needed to be able to tell the differences between letters. They learned to hear the beginning sounds of words and to speak distinctly.

You have much more time with your child. You can easily direct his learning to master the skills he needs for success in school. The next chapter will give you an exact outline to follow.

Chapter 6

How you can prepare your child to read: Preschool years

We saw from Piaget and Montessori that a child needs to learn in two ways. He needs to interact with objects in his environment and have many real-life experiences to develop his thinking and reasoning powers. At the same time, he needs to hear words that label these objects and experiences so he can recall and build on the concepts that he formulates. Both kinds of learning must occur for the child to reach the level of abstract thinking that he needs to be able to read.

In the last chapter, we saw how the basic intelligence of a child increases with his active participation every day. In a general way, we saw the skills that he needs to prepare him to read. But now that you're going to be teaching these skills in your own home, I have listed the most important ones in figure 6-1 so you can keep them in mind as you read this chapter.

We can easily provide opportunities to insure that our child will learn these skills. First, we must use our homes and neighborhoods as a learning environment. Second, we must talk and read to our child so that he hears and uses many words. Gradually, he'll build a foundation for reading.

Real-life activities

When my son was one-and-a-half years old, he took the pans out and then fitted their covers on them. If he had a chance, he emptied the

---

To become ready to read, a child must be able to:

- name objects, actions, textures, sizes, numbers, colors, and shapes
- recognize rhyming patterns
- follow two-step directions
- understand complex sentences

Figure 6-1 Pre-reading skills

contents of the cereal boxes and the sugar bowls and the salt and pepper shakers. He dumped out ashtrays, poured out perfume bottles, sprinkled powder from boxes. He ate the dog food and put a hairpin in the electrical socket.

When he was two years old, he loved to stand at the kitchen sink and play in the water with measuring cups, a funnel, a strainer, and other household items. He loved to put plastic and wooden spoons in the water and watch them float and sink.

At two-and-a-half years old, he took all the clothes out of his drawers and carefully put them back again. This occupied him for a long time. Now, he could follow directions to put them back in order—the socks in one drawer, the underpants in another, etc.

He could go from room to room and collect all the wastebaskets for me and empty them into a large plastic trash bag. He could put his books back on the shelf. He could sort his blocks from his puzzles.

He investigated and explored. He made discoveries when he mixed materials together, like catsup and milk. He observed cause and effect when he blew bubbles into his drink with his straw. He practiced writing with soapy fingers on the bathroom wall when he took his bath.

He was never interested in toys. He didn't like to "play." He loved to help me. He liked to vacuum and dust, sweep and rake, scrub and polish.

Frankly, at the time I didn't understand his behavior. But now I know he was being a typical preschooler; he was experimenting and learning from his everyday experiences.

Real-life activities teach the child in several ways. They give him a chance to use his muscles and coordinate his eyes and hands. They let him experiment with new materials and formulate ideas about these materials. They show him something about the order and reversibility in nature. And if an adult shares the activities with him, the child learns words that give meaning to his experiences.

For example, when he takes a bath, a child experiments with water. His first observations of the natural properties of water derive from his physical contact with it. If he has cups of different sizes and shapes, he sees that liquid pours and changes its form. If he pours with a pitcher, a funnel, a sieve, and a baster, he gains a deeper understanding of the characteristics of water. When he "plays" with his bath toys, he notices that some objects float and others sink. From an everyday activity, he learns an infinite amount about his environment.

Later on, when he helps you wash the car, he observes other characteristics of water and soap. He makes new discoveries when he sees and feels the differences in the metal of the car, the glass of the window, the rubber of the hose and the tires, the plastic of the bucket and the sponge, and the cotton of the drying cloth. He learns how to squeeze the sponge, grasp the hose, and scrub with a circular motion. He adds words to his vocabulary as he listens and follows your directions. He sees the step-by-step order of the process and the end result of his labors.

Similar observations and growth occur when your child washes the outdoor furniture, waters the flowers, or clips the grass along the walkway. Let him wash the dishes, dust the furniture, and vacuum the rug. When he shops with you at the supermarket, let him help you load the cart, carry the packages, and unpack them in the cupboards at home. With each activity, he has an opportunity to record new observations, to pay attention to different aspects of the same material, to learn new muscular behaviors, to look at new substances, and to organize his world with language.

Toys teach too

Toys are additional learning tools for a child. His play extends the growth of his intelligence. But you must put some thought into choosing toys that will teach your child what you want him to know.

Limit the playthings in your home to those that develop a specific skill. Your child's toys should contribute to the development of his thought and language. They should increase his auditory, visual, and tactile perceptions.

Too many toys confuse and distract. The child tends to move from one to another, never getting deeply involved with any. To build a longer attention span, have only those materials that interest your child and teach him.

In his room or play corner, have a place for everything. Use old shoeboxes or plastic dishpans to hold blocks and puzzles. Don't have a toy box and throw everything in together. When he learns to keep the pieces of a puzzle together or to separate his blocks from his cars, he learns the meaning of *same* and *different*. He begins to classify objects. Help him to see the order in life.

Blocks

Your child should have a set of geometric wooden blocks. They afford opportunities for creative imaginative play and give him tactile experiences with shapes. With them he can make a garage, a house, an airport, a train, or anything he imagines.

As he "plays," he observes new concepts. When your child builds a tower, he sees an orderly progression. He can understand *tall* and *taller*, *high* and *higher*. When he knocks the blocks down, he observes a phenomenon of nature—the pull of gravity. He needs to do it again and again to know that this will always happen.

Geometric blocks also train the child's eye to notice shapes in his surroundings. He can experiment with the special features of each shape. Cylinders roll. Four triangles fit together to make a square:

Two squares make a rectangle:

Blocks and cylinders of graduated sizes help your child see size relationships. Plastic nesting cubes of different sizes that fit within each other and stack in a pyramid tower provide an exercise that he'll experiment with for years (see figure 6-2). As he holds the different blocks in his hands, he forms an understanding of size— *large*, *small*, *larger*, *smaller*.

Figure 6-2   Learning tower

Other manipulatives

Wooden beads and laces like those shown in figure 6-3 develop hand-eye coordination and visual perception. As your child puts the different colored beads on the string, he can make a pattern. For example, he may alternate red, blue, yellow, and green until he has used all the beads in the set. Or he can place them according to their round, oval, and square shapes to create other designs. He can also match the beads to a card with a pattern on it that you can buy or make.

Other toys that improve the child's ability to notice similarities and differences in colors and shapes include pegboards, play tiles, and wooden cube and parquetry design blocks (see figure 6-4). You might even want to invest in my favorites, cube and parquetry

Figure 6-3 Beads and laces

design boards so your child can match the blocks to the pattern on a card. All these different-colored blocks and manipulatives develop concepts of color and shape.

Puzzles

Puzzles also train the eye. They help a child see other attributes of a common item. When your child is very young, choose those that are wholes and have distinctive outlines. For example, the first puzzle shown in figure 6-5 is one I've used with young children because it has only fruits. Later on, buy those that have logical divisions, like the second puzzle in figure 6-5; these help your child see part-to-whole relationships. Always try to determine what the puzzle will teach your child.

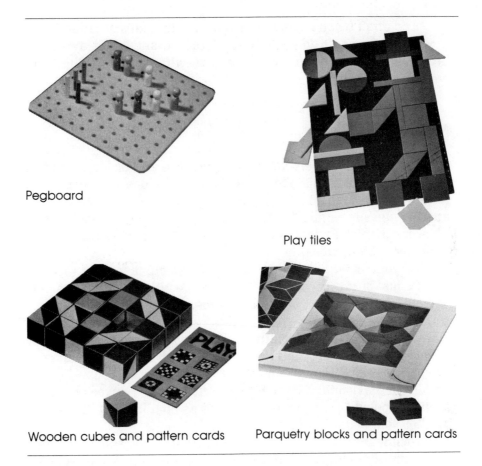

Pegboard

Play tiles

Wooden cubes and pattern cards   Parquetry blocks and pattern cards

Figure 6-4   Other size and shape manipulatives that teach your child

Figure 6-5   Choose puzzles that will train your child's eye

And don't frustrate him with a puzzle that he's not ready to do. If you find he can't do it, help him finish it, and put it away until he's ready for it. Don't confuse him with a puzzle that's too complicated.

Math toys

Mathematical skills help your child measure and order the objects in his world. From his observations, he develops the concepts of large and small, short and tall, thick and thin. The pitcher is large and the glass is small. The teddy bear is tall and the doll is short. The rope is thick and the string is thin. He compares and contrasts the objects he handles.

As your child gets older, a cloth or steel measuring tape will satisfy his curiosity about length and width. Let him measure objects—tables, doors, etc.—to increase his perceptions of size.

Teach your child to count and to recognize numbers. Give him many opportunities to learn them. One way is to write the numbers in the sections of an egg carton. Begin with zero and number to eleven. To teach him the meaning of zero, have your child put nothing in that section. Have him put one penny or poker chip in the section labeled "1"; two pennies in the section labeled "2"; and on until eleven.

He'll want to play with this often. He'll do the same procedure again and again to gain an understanding of each number. When he knows how to count, he'll count his cars, blocks, books, etc. This gives him a number concept—a true meaning of what the symbol represents.

He'll also discover other characteristics of numbers as he rearranges these objects during his "play" time. For example, when he places eight poker chips in a circle, he'll find he has the same number as when he stretches them out in a straight line:

He'll begin to understand conservation of material—that the arrangement of items doesn't affect the number.

Classification

Besides teaching your child his numbers, egg cartons can also be used to classify objects. Let your child sort buttons in an egg carton. (You can buy an odd lot assortment of buttons at a fabric shop for a small fee.) When he separates buttons, shells, stones, and any small collection by color, size, or shape, he sees the differences within a class of objects. If you blindfold him and he sorts by feeling the outline, he improves his sense of touch. Muffin tins and plastic margarine or cottage cheese containers can also be used to sort objects.

School-type activities

Real-life activities and working with different objects and materials in the home build thinking and perceptual skills. Direct school-oriented experiences also prepare a child to write and read. Supervise and plan times for your child to make shapes with clay, to cut with a scissors, to paint with watercolors, to scribble with markers, to draw with stencils. Your child needs many experiences with all these mediums to build small muscle coordination.

Clay is a plastic material that fascinates children because it changes its shape. With their fingers, they can roll it, pat it, pound it. They can cut it into pieces with a wooden popsicle stick. They can shape it into a ball or a sausage. They can make donuts, snakes, or animals.

You can make your own clay dough as follows:

1. Mix 1-1/2 cups flour and 1/2 cup salt in a bowl.
2. Slowly add 1/2 cup water and 1/4 cup vegetable oil or a few drops of liquid detergent.
3. Knead dough well and shape into balls.

NOTE: If the dough becomes too sticky, add more flour. If it's too dry, add more water.

This recipe is enough for two people.

Another easy-to-make item is paste:

1.   Combine 1 cup flour and 1/2 cup water until creamy.
2.   Store in a covered container.

You can use this paste for a variety of activities. For example, you can help your child make his own picture book. Let him cut pictures from old magazines and paste them on sheets of paper. With paper fasteners, you can easily assemble a book.

To give him more practice with scissors and paste, let him make a collage with pictures he cuts out. Or have him design pictures with scraps of wallpaper or cloth, bits of yarn, or colored tissue paper. Old wrapping paper, ribbon, and greeting cards are other sources for your child's creativity.

Stencils provide another creative outlet for your child as they teach him shapes and small muscle coordination. You can make a set of your own from cardboard. Just cut out basic shapes; then let your child trace and color with them. At first, he'll trace a simple outline:

As his skills and perceptions improve, he'll use the shapes to produce more complicated drawings:

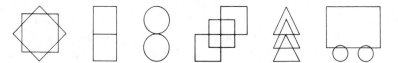

With markers and watercolors, he can be even more creative. When he tries to put on paper the things that he sees in his world, he must pay attention to details of color, size, shape, and number. For example, if he wants to draw a tree, he must think that it has one large, straight brown trunk and several smaller, twisted brown branches. It also has many small, irregularly-shaped leaves of several different shades of green. He must integrate or unite all his experiences with trees into one picture of a tree. Painting and drawing force the child to bring all the parts together as they let him examine other materials.

Let him experiment

You'll find that your child is content and happy to experiment with the same activities again and again. He'll choose those that allow him to grow in his skills. Mechanical toys that require him to be an observer rather than a participant won't hold his attention for long.

As his teacher, you should stimulate and guide his learning. Observe his progress. Notice his needs. Add new materials when he shows that he's ready. Show him new techniques to imitate. Set up an activity and let him experiment. He'll teach himself.

In short, make your relationship with your child a happy one by recognizing that he learns from every experience. Have patience and permit him to explore at his own pace. Encourage him to follow his curious impulses by providing an environment with safe, durable materials and objects that can be used in many ways. Remember that you don't need to spend a lot of money—use the resources in your own home to expand your child's intelligence.

Give him language

Language develops spontaneously. As the child makes mathematical and scientific discoveries about his surroundings from his experiences, he absorbs words. If you enjoy your child and talk to him, his knowledge of words just naturally increases. You elaborate and extend his language in your daily associations with him.

Your child needs to learn three specific kinds of language before he begins to read. First, he should know the names for objects and actions in his environment. Next, he should be able to recognize rhyming patterns. Finally, he should be familiar with written sentence structure and vocabulary.

Talk to him

Your child follows three sequential steps when he learns the language that relates to objects. First, he recognizes and remembers the name or label for the object when you say it. Next, he learns to select the correct object from a group when you say the name to him. For example, when you say, "Give me the red one," he finds it for you. Finally, he's able to recall the name from his memory bank and say it when you ask him, "What is this?"

When you talk to your child, you provide the labels that organize and classify his world. You begin with those that permit him to satisfy his basic needs—*water, milk, cracker.* Then, you add phrases and sentences.

As his language grows, you share your feelings with him. "I'm sad because Grandpa has the flu." "I'm happy because I'm going to the ball game." "I'll be late to meet Mommy if I don't hurry." And you help him to express his feelings. "You're angry." "You're hungry." "You're tired."

When you go to the park and the supermarket and the zoo, you give him other new words. When you show him the object and then give him the word, he gets a full understanding of the language.

So when you walk to the park, supply words for the things that he sees along the way. *Bird, squirrel, leaf, flower*—let him name the objects in the neighborhood. Use few words so you don't confuse him. Your child will naturally imitate your speech and learn automatically if you speak clearly and enunciate carefully.

When you take him to the supermarket, talk to him as you move through the store. "I'm going to buy some vegetables. ... Now we're ready to go to the cashier."

When you go to the zoo, tell him the names of the animals. Point out their distinguishing characteristics, the differences in the kinds of houses they live in, and the kinds of foods they eat. "Seals have shiny black skin, need water to live in, and eat fish. Tigers have orange and black fur, live in the jungle, and walk like cats."

Your child understands many words that he doesn't speak. Encourage him to recall these labels. When I taught preschool, I would sit with a child when he did a puzzle (or any other learning activity). Then, I would hold up a piece of the puzzle, such as an animal, and ask him, "What is this called?" If he gave me a blank stare that indicated he didn't know the name of the animal, I told him. "This is a zebra." It wasn't long before the child responded with the words he had learned.

When your child strings beads, you can ask him, "What color is this?" or "What shape is this?" He'll ask you the same questions as he learns this sentence structure. He mimics these forms to practice them. When you answer him, you reinforce his knowledge. In this way, you also teach him that these are important things to know.

When you ask your child to follow your verbal directions, you also require him to show that he understands. For example, when you ask him, "Please bring me the baby's sweater. It's upstairs on the bed," he must understand the meanings of all the words. He must remember what it is you want and where to go to find it.

Read to him

When you talk to your child and encourage him to talk to you, he learns the language that he uses every day. When you read to him, you introduce him to words that are not part of his daily life. Thus, reading is an important tool for teaching your child the naming vocabulary he needs to become a good reader himself.

Set a regular time to read every day so your child looks forward to it as something special. I never had trouble getting my children to go to bed at night because a bedtime story was part of their evening ritual. A routine provides a pleasant association with reading from the earliest days of your child's life. When you hold him and cuddle him as you read, you give him positive feelings about books.

Read to him before he starts to talk. Show your child picture books from the time he is a year old. He understands a great deal of language before he uses words himself.

The alphabet books that later teach the letters can be used from the beginning of your reading to teach words. Point to the picture as you say the name of the object so that he sees a direct connection.

As your child gets more advanced in his language and can say the words to you, introduce him to *Richard Scarry's Best Word Book Ever*. This will familiarize him with the names of more than 1,400 objects. It has full-color illustrations of items in the home and the neighborhood—the park, the farm, the airport, the garden, etc. It helps the child organize his world with language.

My Weekly Reader Picture Word Book will also increase your child's labeling vocabulary and help him classify the items in his environment. It too presents words in groups—people, animals, toys, seasons, etc. In addition, there are stories, word games, puzzles, riddles, and rhymes that make your child think. Throughout the book, questions ask him about what he sees on the pages.

Richard Scarry's Best Counting Book Ever will teach him to count. It contributes to an understanding of numbers as it asks the child to count the wheels on a scooter and a tricycle, the number of bunnies and firetrucks, the number of mice and racing cars. It provides many opportunities to see number relationships.

Rhyming words

The English language is composed of words that rhyme. From very simple roots, more complex words are formed. For example, *an* changes to *can, fan, man, ran. And* becomes *bland, stand, command, contraband.* So the second language skill your child needs before learning to read is to be able to hear these similarities and differences in sound.

The best way to teach rhyming is to read Mother Goose. Children love the nonsense poems and the pictures. They love to hear the same sound repeated at the beginning of words, such as "The Muffin Man" and "Pease Porridge Hot." They love the repetition of phrases, as in "London Bridge is falling down, falling down, falling down."

With Mother Goose rhymes, they quickly learn to differentiate between the sounds of letters. What better way to become aware of the sound *p* than "Peter Piper Picked a Peck of Pickled Peppers?" For *s* there's "Simple Simon"; for *w,* "Wee Willie Winkie"; for *d,* "Deedle, Deedle, Dumpling."

Mother Goose will also train your child's memory. You and your child can recall these rhymes in the car on the way to the supermarket or on the bus to the doctor's office. The imagery is so vivid that the poems are easy to memorize. Who can forget Little Miss Muffet and the spider or Humpty Dumpty's fall? When your child sees how pleased you are with his recitation, he sees that you like him to learn words. This also contributes to his good feelings about himself.

The pictures in Mother Goose books continue to reinforce the naming vocabulary of your child as they add unusual words that aren't part of his everyday life. Some examples are *cupboard* from "Old Mother Hubbard"; *cobbler* from "Cobbler, Cobbler, Mend My Shoe"; and *scholar* from "A Diller, A Dollar."

Mother Goose also teaches correct sentence structure and action verbs. One of the language tests I've given to kindergarten children evaluates their proper use of verb tenses. Many don't know the irregular forms, such as *go, went, have gone; fall, fell, have fallen; break, broke, have broken.* Children can't learn these patterns unless they hear them frequently. Mother Goose rhymes are full of them and of many less common verbs as well:

> Jack and Jill
> *Went* up the hill
> To *fetch* a pail of water;
> Jack *fell* down,
> And *broke* his crown,
> And Jill came *tumbling* after.

The rhymes also teach children some of the concepts that are a part of everyday life. For example, here's one that teaches rote counting:

> One, two, three, four, and five,
> I caught a hare alive,
> Six, seven, eight, nine, and ten,
> I let him go again.

And this one teaches time sequence:

> As Tommy Snooks and Bessy Brooks
> Were walking out on Sunday,
> Said Tommy Snooks to Bessy Brooks
> "Tomorrow will be Monday."

So use Mother Goose to teach your child rhyming patterns, sound recognition, new vocabulary, proper language usage, and everyday concepts that help him recognize the order in his world—all of which prepare him to learn to read.

Records

After your child knows some of the Mother Goose rhymes, he'll be fascinated to hear someone else say them on a record ... and he'll be able to join in reciting them. An inexpensive record player is all you need, and you can borrow records from the library.

Music should be a part of your child's life. It trains his ear to recognize different sounds better than any other auditory exercise. With his natural imitation, he tries to reproduce the sounds that he hears. Language learning is easy and effortless with music.

Ella Jenkins sings and plays a guitar in a way that endears her to all young children. She has a collection of records for Folkway Records that develop language and listening skills. She talks to children in a real way and sings traditional and original songs that have a lot of repetition. She has a gentle, patient way that invites the child to participate. She holds the child's attention with her easy, relaxed style and natural rhythm. Her warmth and love for children radiate through all her albums.

Begin with "Nursery Rhymes." In this album, Ella Jenkins sings and recites all the favorites. She sings or says the rhymes twice, using a different inflection each time. Sometimes, she hums the rhyme. Sometimes, she recites it and asks the child to finish the last word of each line. As he listens and joins in, your child will extend his attention span and develop his expression and rhythm in reciting.

Children from a nursery school join Ella Jenkins on "Rhythm and Game Songs for the Little Ones." This album was especially created for preschoolers as a teaching aid for parents and teachers. Your child will want to clap his hands, walk, stamp his feet, tiptoe, jump, skip, and hop in rhythm to the music as directed. He'll want to imitate Miss Jenkins when she changes her voice during the song, "It's the Milkman."

"This is Rhythm" presents a variety of musical instruments that help your child tune in to different sounds. On Side One, Ella Jenkins explains rhythm and changes the melody on the piano to simulate a heartbeat, a top spinning, footsteps, and many other rhythms in the everyday world. On Side Two, she sings songs that illustrate different rhythms.

"My Street Begins at My House" is especially good for rainy days because she sings "Rain, Rain, Go Away" and plays easy, quiet games, including a unique one to sing called "It's Raining Cats and Dogs." Children listen and follow her directions that require them to move and think.

Pete Seeger's "American Folk Songs for Children" is especially suited for two- and three-year-olds. Folk music has been a natural part of the daily lives of Americans in different parts of the country. It has simple narratives and varied rhythms. The repetition of the lyrics, the easy rhythms, and the simplicity of the subject matter invite children to sing along with "This Old Man," "Frog Went A-Courting," "Train is A-Coming," and "Bought Me a Cat."

Tom Glazer is a balladeer who sings and talks clearly and directly to children. He has three volumes of "Activity and Game Songs" that will extend your child's language and memory. In these albums, Tom Glazer leads hundreds of children in folk songs and games that teach.

These three artists incorporate the important elements of education in their music. They motivate the child with material that reflects his interest and is easy for him to understand. They invite the child to join in so he can learn by doing. They satisfy his need for repetition and movement.

The language of books

The third language skill your child needs before learning how to read is to know the kind of language that's printed in books. Here,

I'm not talking about the simple alphabet and labeling books I mentioned earlier in this chapter but about books that tell a complete story using a variety of vocabulary and sentence structures. It's important for your child to know sentences that are more complex and words that go beyond the normal, everyday speaking vocabulary. If your child doesn't understand these literary structures and words, he'll learn to read, but later, he won't understand what he's reading.

To prepare your child and to give him an enjoyment of literature, read him the stories that are classics. Your child should be acquainted with *The Three Billy Goats Gruff*, *The Three Bears*, *The Three Little Pigs*, *Cinderella*, *King Midas and the Golden Touch*, *Peter Rabbit*, *The Little Red Hen*, and *The Gingerbread Boy*. All have simple language, easy narratives, and lots of repetition. They offer fantasy that satisfies the child's imagination.

They also teach him to follow the natural order of events. Have your child tell you the step-by-step progression of one of these stories while you're driving in the car or sitting in an office waiting room. You may be surprised to hear him acting out the roles of the big bad wolf and the three little pigs as he swings by himself at the park or digs alone in the sandbox.

Other than the classics, my favorites for language development, and later, beginning reading, are the Beginner Books by Random House. *I Wish That I Had Duck Feet* and *The Best Nest* are two sensitive, imaginative stories that have appealed to every child in my experience. They have rich rhyming patterns and hold the child's attention with an uncomplicated story line.

Some recent books have become classics in children's literature because they reflect real concerns and interests of children. Ezra Jack Keats illustrates and writes books that children love. His drawings are childlike in their colorful simplicity. His sentences are succinct and graphic. His stories are clear narratives of children's experiences.

The Trip relates an account of a child in a new neighborhood with no friends who takes an unusual, pretend trip to his old neighborhood. *Peter's Chair* tells how a boy feels about a new baby sister and how he adjusts to the changes she causes in his life. *Whistle for Willie* describes the feelings of a boy who wishes he could whistle. *The Snowy Day* recounts the activities of a boy on the first day of snow of the season. Your child will learn from these and many more books by Ezra Jack Keats.

Animal stories also have great appeal for children. *Clifford, the Big Red Dog* by Norman Bridwell is a tale of a dog who grows bigger because his mistress tells him that she loves him. This fantasy causes even very young children to listen attentively as the little puppy becomes an enormous dog. It expresses the child's own desires to be loved and to grow bigger. After this initial meeting, your child will also enjoy further humorous stories about Clifford.

H. A. Rey created the *Curious George* series. These adventures of a monkey who gets into mischief delight children. The sentences are simple; the language is descriptive; the plots are humorous; and the illustrations of the animals and people are happy and lovable.

Bernard Waber's *Lyle, Lyle Crocodile* series is just as well-liked. The vocabulary and sentence structure are slightly more complex, but Lyle's antics touch and amuse children as much.

Make Way for Ducklings by Robert McCloskey is another animal story that children love. They identify with the problems the parent ducks have in finding a place to nest and raise their brood. The pictures are charming, and the language is descriptive and rhythmic.

These books hold a child's attention. They provide models for standard English sentence structure. They introduce new vocabulary that's not commonly heard in the home. They show children that books are a source of pleasure.

Children delight in hearing the same books over and over again. Just as they learn something new each succeeding time they put a puzzle together, so they absorb more language each time they hear the same story repeated. Linguists and reading specialists agree that being able to read depends on the ability to understand and produce the spoken language. If you read these stories, they'll provide a foundation for reading.

Create an environment that teaches the skills your child needs to be able to read. Talk and listen to him so he develops a good oral vocabulary. Read to your child what you enjoy, and you'll impart to him a love of literature. Read to him what he enjoys, and he'll be motivated to learn to read for himself.

Chapter 7

How I taught 20 city first graders to read

The 20 children in my first-grade class were of many racial, ethnic, and cultural backgrounds. Eleven were white, six were black, two were Hispanic, and one was from Thailand.

Not one child came in reading. Most of them knew most letters and sounds in the beginning of the year. All of them knew the sounds for A, M, P, C, N, and T. But none of them could read.

At the end of the school year, nine scored above second-grade level on the Iowa Basic Skills Test, a nationally standardized achievement test. The highest score was 2.7 (second grade, seventh month). Five scored between 1.6 and 1.9. One boy who needed glasses scored 1.5, and one boy in bilingual education scored 1.2. Two did not get a reading score because they were too slow and the Iowa test is a timed test. These two recorded 2.0 and 2.2 on word analysis and 1.3 and 1.6 on spelling, however. (The two remaining children didn't take this particular test because I felt they were too immature emotionally and the testing would cause them too much stress. Their progress was definitely slower than the rest, though by the end of the year they passed the Chicago Board of Education skill tests for beginning reading.)

What did I do?

Everything I did in the classroom from September through June was planned to give the children the message that they could learn to read. I used every activity in art, math, social studies, science, and music to show them that reading is getting meaning from print and that it's easy and fun.

My formula was simple and it worked. First, I continually showed them the connection between speech and print. Second, I made sure that they knew the names for the letters. Third, I taught them the most common sound for each letter. Fourth, I taught them to recognize some of the most often-used words. Last, I had them read, read, read.

How did I do it?

I used praise and approval every day. The children needed to know I was pleased by their efforts and accomplishments so they'd be motivated to learn more.

But praise alone didn't always work at first. Some of the children wouldn't even try to pay attention. For quite a few, praise by itself just wasn't a reward. But for all at the start of the school year, the promise of a tiny piece of candy was enough to keep them sitting quietly for a lesson in letters and sounds. (Before I could teach them anything, I had to have their attention.)

Curiosity motivates some children to listen and learn. But by the time most children reach first grade, they've decided that school is something they must endure. They don't expect it to be fun. They expect to be interrupted by someone just when they're interested. They expect to be asked to "be quiet" just when they feel like talking about what they see in class. They expect to hear the same things they've heard before. They need to know that learning can be meaningful. That's why we must praise and reward children when they do listen to us so they'll want to do it again.

For example, one thing I did at the beginning of the year was to take special note of the children who did listen and learn. This helped get the attention of those who couldn't seem to sit still and tune in. Children are always interested in their peers and they love to please. So when they hear that someone else is doing the right thing, they take particular notice of it and try to copy it. As soon as one of these other children was quiet, I praised him for his effort until they all sat still and listened.

When I had everyone's attention, I made it worthwhile for them. I either taught them something meaningful, showed them something pleasurable, or talked about something interesting. In time they all sat quietly whenever I told them, "I have something important to tell you" or "I have a story I want to read to you."

When they could remember what I asked them to learn, I expressed great delight. Sometimes I pretended to be really surprised that they had mastered the task. Sometimes, if it was a difficult skill that had taken them a long time, I gave them a football card or special Snoopy pencil. Eventually, reading became its own reward.

Connection between speech and print

I read books to them every day—books that they could quickly learn to read themselves. I used the Random House Beginner Books. In the upper righthand corner of each book is a Cat in the Hat with the words "I CAN READ IT ALL BY MYSELF." And every time I read one of these books, I showed them that emblem.

With my finger, I pointed to each word in the title and on the pages inside the books. I wanted them to see that I was getting meaning from the printed symbols. I wanted them to see the connection between the letters on the page and the words I said. They needed to know that I was doing something specific when I read. It wasn't magic!

Some of the books were very simple like *Go, Dog, Go* and *Ten Apples Up On Top*. Some of the books had more subtle encouragement like the *Diggingest Dog*, which is about a dog who has to try to do something he's never tried before. All of these books appealed to their imagination and their interest. I had no problem gaining every child's attention when I reached for a book from my special shelf. (And I always told them that these were my own special books.)

I showed them that reading was fun. I enjoyed all the books I read—and only read books that I was enthusiastic about. I laughed heartily when the story was humorous and displayed sorrow when it was sad. I conveyed to them that I thought reading was the greatest pleasure you could have.

I told them that reading was talk-written-down; that everything they could say could be written and read later by anyone who had certain definite skills that they too could learn.

Letters and sounds

I told them that reading was not a guessing game. I made them understand and repeat back to me that there are 26 letters in the alphabet—26 large and 26 small letters—and each has a name and a sound of its own.

In kindergarten, they should have learned to recognize the letters, and some of them had. But they needed to know the letter-names as well as they knew their own names. To be able to read, they also needed to know that each letter has its own sound.

In the beginning of the year, especially, I stressed individual letter-sound relationships. Once a week, I read an alphabet picture book. My favorite is *Dr. Seuss's ABC* because it's very simple and repetitive. For example:

> BIG A
> little a
> What begins with A?
> Aunt Annie's alligator ... A .. a .. A

There is no question about what it's teaching—the name of the letter and the sound the letter represents.

Then I had them write the letters—upper and lowercase together—and draw a picture to stand for the sound of each letter, as shown in figure 7-1. (Some children feel they cannot draw. I wanted all my students to know they could do this, so I showed them how to make drawings with easy outlines.) The more advanced children made more than one picture for each letter. If their language was elaborate, they drew a library for *L* and a policeman for *P*.

The child must have a complete, total, immersed understanding of this continuity between letters and sounds. He must have an automatic sound association for the letter when he sees it. That's why we did the same thing week after week until some recited the entire ABC book from memory and could draw pictures for all 26 letters in 20 minutes. No one ever said, "Oh no, not again!"

Every day for their seat work, while I took a small "reading group," I had them practice writing a letter—upper and lowercase—on ruled paper, as shown in figure 7-2. I also had them do a picture/letter paper on the same letter, like the one in figure 7-3. They had to write the letter that corresponded to the beginning sound of each picture.

This strengthened their naming vocabulary as it reinforced their letter-sound associations. I was surprised that many children didn't know a gate from a fence or the difference between a duck and a goose. So often we're teaching more than one thing at a time. It's frequently hard to determine where the child is having a problem.

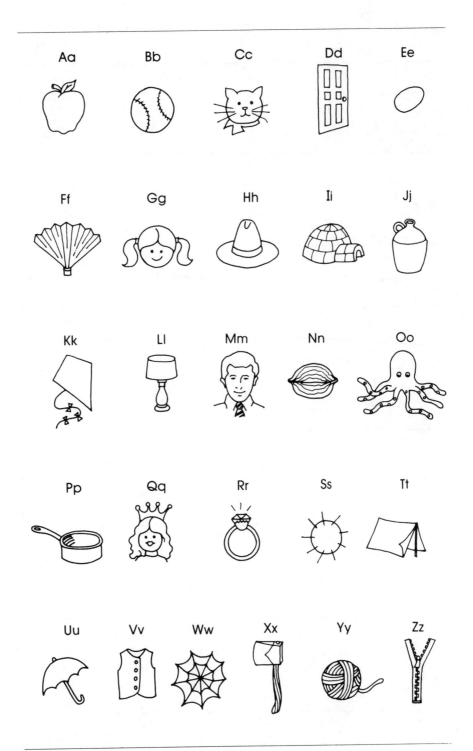

Figure 7-1 Alphabet pictures

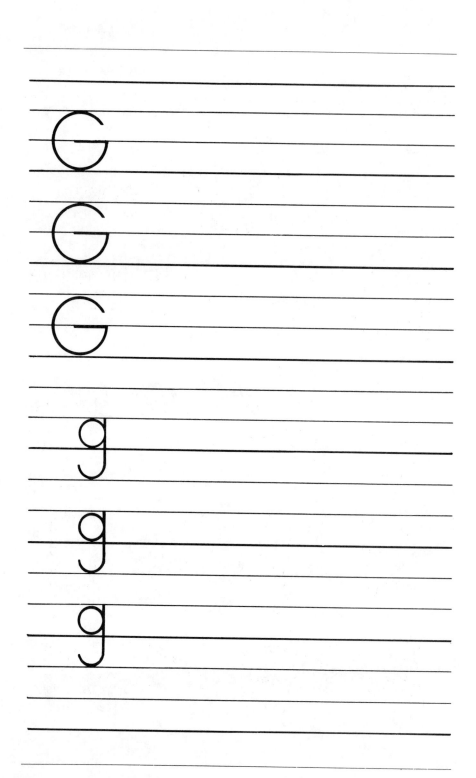

Figure 7-2 Letter practice sheet

Figure 7-3   Letter–sound sheet

As their reward for doing this drill, the third paper that they did every day was a color-by-number that trained their eyes to see shapes and taught them to recognize the words for the colors. These papers were easy in the beginning of the year with large outlines (see figure 7-4) and became more complicated as the year went on (see figure 7-5). This exercise also showed them the connection between speech and print. The color names were printed on the crayons, and they could match them to the words on the papers.

Sight words

At first they said, "I can't read." And I stressed that they could. I showed them that they already knew two words, *I* and *a*. But they also needed to know that several letters together make words. So I wrote the following words on 4 x 6 cards:

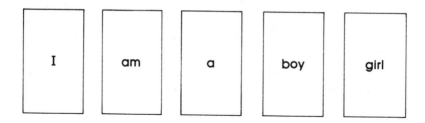

Then I made the sentences "I am a boy" and "I am a girl" by changing the word card at the end.

Reading is a combination of decoding skills and the ability to recognize sight words ... words that don't follow the regular letter-sound relationships. To teach the children these skills, I now began to add word cards for some of the words shown in figure 7-6. The 220 words listed there have been selected as the most often-used words in English speech and writing. As you can see, some of them closely correspond to the letter-sound relationships, while others are irregular. If a child knows all of them, he can read on the third-grade level.

I chose some of the most common words on the list to teach next: *in, is, it, at, an,* and *the.* On one side of the word card, I printed the word beginning with a capital letter so the children could learn to recognize the word at the beginning of a sentence. On the other side of the card, I printed the word in all lowercase letters:

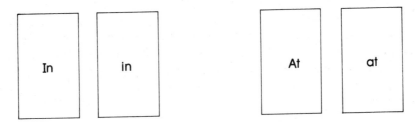

I told them they would find these words everywhere—in the newspapers, in magazines, on street signs, etc. If they could read in school, they could read anywhere.

I will always remember the quiet little boy who brought his book to me and gently tapped my arm. "Look," he said with a beautiful, surprised smile as he pointed to *the*. "There is that word you taught us."

Next, I showed them that when you put another letter in front of these words, you make new words. *An* becomes *can, fan, man, pan, ran,* and *tan. At* becomes *cat, fat, hat, mat, pat, rat,* and *sat. In* becomes *bin, fin, pin, tin,* and *win. It* becomes *bit, fit, hit, lit, pit,* and *sit.*

I made more word cards. On one side, I wrote the root word; on the other side, I wrote the new words:

an	can fan man pan ran tan		at	cat fat hat mat pat rat sat
in	bin fin pin tin win		it	bit fit hit lit pit sit

This way they combined the skills of sight recognition and letter-sound association.

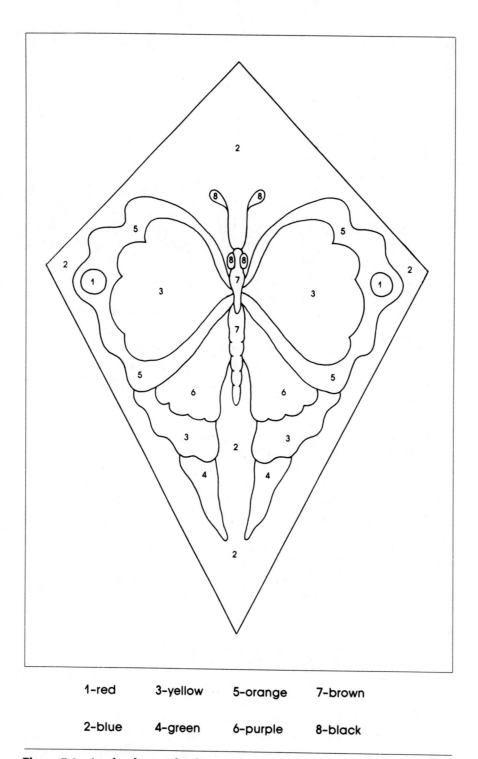

| 1-red | 3-yellow | 5-orange | 7-brown |
| 2-blue | 4-green | 6-purple | 8-black |

Figure 7-4 A color–by–number kite

1-brown   3-green   5-blue

2-black   4-purple   6-red

Figure 7-5   A color-by-number dog

Pre-primer

a	find	is	not	three
and	for	it	one	to
away	funny	jump	play	two
big	go	little	red	up
blue	help	look	run	we
can	here	make	said	where
come	I	me	see	yellow
down	in	my	the	you

Primer

all	do	no	she	well
am	eat	now	so	went
are	four	on	soon	what
at	get	our	that	white
ate	good	out	there	who
be	have	please	they	will
black	he	pretty	this	with
brown	into	ran	too	yes
but	like	ride	under	
came	must	saw	want	
did	new	say	was	

First grade

after	fly	how	open	then
again	from	just	over	there
an	give	know	put	think
any	going	let	round	walk
as	had	live	some	when
ask	has	may	stop	
by	her	of	take	
could	him	old	thank	
every	his	once	them	

Figure 7-6 Dolch basic word list (part 1 of 2)

Second grade

always	does	made	tell	why
around	don't	many	their	wish
because	fast	off	these	work
been	first	or	those	would
before	five	pull	upon	write
best	found	read	us	your
both	gave	right	use	
buy	goes	sing	very	
call	green	sit	wash	
cold	its	sleep	which	

Third grade

about	eight	if	only	ten
better	fall	keep	own	today
bring	far	kind	pick	together
carry	full	laugh	seven	try
clean	got	light	shall	warm
cut	grow	long	show	
done	hold	much	six	
draw	hot	myself	small	
drink	hurt	never	start	

Figure 7-6   Dolch basic word list (part 2 of 2)

With these words, the children could read many sentences. Now, to continue to reinforce that reading is fun and to give them a chance to use their new skills, I made worksheets with directions to follow. The simplest began with "I am a man." They had to draw a picture for the sentence. (See figure 7-7.) Later in the year, the directions required more reading and, sometimes, more than one step: "Make a cake. Put a candle on it." (See figure 7-8.)

For my reading groups, I used the Sullivan Associates Programmed Reading Series, available to parents through the Webster Division of McGraw-Hill. It's called "programmed" because it's designed to immediately reinforce the response of the reader. The

I am a man.   I am a can.

This is a cat.   This is a bat.

Here is a pan.   Here is a fan.

The mat is red.   The hat is green.

Figure 7-7 Simple directions to follow in drawing

Put a blue X on
a red ball.

Make a yellow sun.

Put a funny hat here.

This is a red can.

Make a cake. Put a
candle on it.

Draw a tree. Put
apples on it.

Make a man with a
blue hat.

Here is a little ant.
Please stop now.

Figure 7-8 More difficult directions to follow in drawing

workbooks (there are 21 in all) have pictures and sentences in the righthand column of the page and answers in the lefthand column, as shown in figure 7-9. (This is a sample sheet; it's not an actual page from the Sullivan series.)

The child uses a paper slider to cover the answer column in the lefthand margin of the page. He then reads the material on the right side. He either (1) answers the questions with "yes" or "no," (2) chooses the correct word for the sentence, or (3) fills in the blank. When he finishes a section of the page marked by a horizontal line, he moves the slider down to the same horizontal line in the answer column to check whether he did it right or not. If he did it wrong, he changes his response. If he did it right, he is reinforced by seeing his correct answer.

This program is excellent because it's very repetitive and teaches the proper language patterns. It uses the same words that I taught the children, but it puts them in different order: "Is this a cat?"; "Is this a can?" The children loved this repetition and took great pride in completing their workbooks. To them, each workbook marked their progress in reading.

More skills are added with each book in the three-year series. The exercises train the child's eye to see the important changes in the middle of words as well as at the beginning and end. For example, *mat* becomes *met* and *tan* becomes *tin*. Later, *tin* becomes *thin* and then, *chin*. And *pat* becomes *path* and then, *patch*. Children need to notice these important differences if they're going to be able to read on their own.

Write the words

My students' learning was gradual and steady. They began to write and to read.

Every morning they copied a morning story when they came to school. It had basic sight words and the day and the date. The following is a sample:

> Good morning.
> Today is Monday,
> December 15, 1980.
> The sun is out and
> we can go out to play.

The story was nearly the same every day. The children needed the repetition and benefited from it. That became obvious to me one

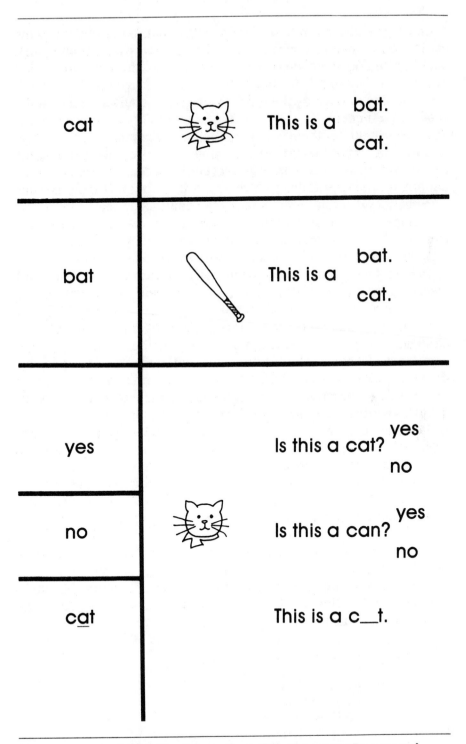

Figure 7-9   A worksheet like those in the Sullivan Associates Programmed
Reading Series

morning when I was late. Before I arrived, a little boy climbed on a chair and put the story on the board. After that, I noticed that many could write their own story from memory. And they spelled words like *Wednesday* and *February* correctly. (I told them that we don't say Wednesday the way it's spelled—that they could sound it out to spell it: *Wed-nes-day*.)

Some children, though, had not had many experiences with letters and as a result could not remember the letters well enough to look at the board and copy the words. For them, I made special papers, and they practiced writing only the letters. If they did this at home too, it wasn't long before they could copy the board.

Some complained that their hands grew tired. I told them to exercise their hand muscles on the bus on the way home and while they watched television at home. I showed them how to stretch and open their fingers and then close them tightly into a fist. After a few weeks, they could see the difference in their work and would proudly bring me their finished papers.

The children practiced writing in many different activities. For example, every month we made our own calendars. This way they saw the order of the days of the week as they learned to spell the days correctly.

For art, we wrote our own little books. For example, we made an alphabet book similar to our original letter/picture exercises in the beginning of the year, only now we added words. (See figure 7-10.)

Children who were unable to do this before they learned some words could now see the connection. They drew pictures for the words that they read in their books and worksheets. All the skills began to come together in one process—reading.

We made a book about Spot, like the one in figure 7-11. And another about spring, as shown in figure 7-12.

The children made cards for all the holidays using stencils that I cut from cardboard. They sounded out words to compose their own messages. Mine usually said, "To my techr—I love you."

Many couldn't hear rhyming words. So we read and recited Mother Goose rhymes to build up their auditory skills. We also sang songs and learned finger plays, such as:

> Open, shut them,
> Open, shut them,
> Give your hands a clap.
> Open, shut them,
> Open, shut them,
> Fold them in your lap.

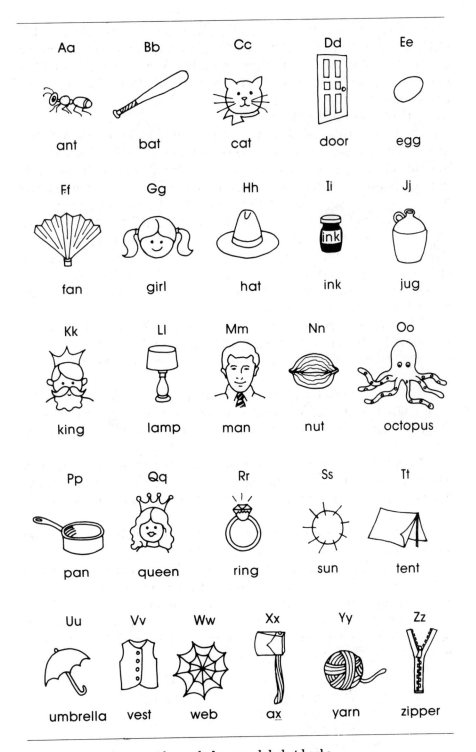

Figure 7-10 Pictures with words for our alphabet books

This is Spot.

This is his house.

He runs and jumps.

He plays with a ball.

I like Spot.

He eats a lot.

Figure 7-11 A book about Spot

**The sun
is out.**

**I see a
butterfly.**

**A bird makes
a nest.**

Flowers grow.

**The grass
comes up.**

**The trees get
leaves.**

Figure 7-12   A book about spring

Sometimes we played a game. I would say a word, such as *mat*. Then, they had to match my word with one that rhymed with it; for example, *pat*, *cat*, *sat*, or *rat*.

We wrote poems as a group so that those who couldn't rhyme could learn from those who did. The following is one of the poems they wrote:

> There once was a cat
> Who was very fat.
> He had very soft fur
> And loved to sit and purr.

Every week we had a spelling test. After the first month, we began with the same simple words that so clearly depict the letter-sound relationships—*a*, *am*, *I*, *mat*, *pan*, *tan*. The message again was clear. "I can write what I can say" and "I can read what I can write."

I added a spelling paper like the one in figure 7-13 to their daily seat work to help them see the order in the language. After they had written these word patterns many times, a child would suddenly come to me and say, "Look, *an* is in all these words." Then I would know that for the first time he really understood the relationships between these words.

At other times, too, the children showed me how they could see the little words in big ones. They pointed out *ant* in *elephant* and *Santa*. They called my attention to *am* in *Abraham* and *in* in *Lincoln* and *Illinois*. They saw *go* in *Chicago* and *ate* in *States*.

I made my own "fill in the blank" sheets with sentences, using the beginning sight words I had taught on the word cards. If the sight word was *hit*, the blank would be a choice of *fit* or *hit*. For example, the first sentence in figure 7-14 is "The bat _____ the ball." (fit, hit). In this way, I showed them that by changing a letter, the word changed. Always, they learned to read by reading.

I created word puzzles similar to the ones that they saw their parents do. (See figure 7-15.) Here the basic sight words were listed as choices for the sentences, just as in the "fill in the blank" exercises. The student had to read the sentence, choose the correct word in context, write it in the blank, and write it again in the puzzle space at the top of the paper. This gave more practice reading and writing.

I also designed other worksheets with riddles, rhyming sentences to complete, and directions to follow. (Figures 7-16 and 7-17 are examples.) Everything in the classroom required them to read and write.

Write 5 times

an

can

fan

man

pan

tan

Figure 7-13 Spelling practice sheet

---

1. The bat _____the ball.
   (fit, hit)

2. My cat ran after the _____.
   (sat, rat)

3. I have a _____ dishpan.
   (pig, big)

4. Can you go on a _____ with me?
   (rip, trip)

5. Stand up and _____ to me.
   (lump, jump)

6. She has my new _____ on.
   (fat, hat)

7. I am going to _____ a cake.
   (make, fake)

8. It will be a good _____.
   (rake, cake)

9. I will eat it so _____.
   (fast, past)

10. I can come and _____ with you.
    (sing, ding)

Figure 7-14 Fill in the blanks

Reading for pleasure

I told them it was work to learn what you needed to know to read, but it was something you wanted to do. The pleasure of reading was a reward for the drills. When they finished their work—morning story, reading worksheets, math activities, etc.—they could get a book and read. At the end of the day, they could sign out a book on my clipboard. (They had to copy the title themselves and sign their own name.) They could read on the bus on the way home, and later, to their parents or siblings who would listen.

As some became fluent readers, the others were motivated to learn. Now my new readers told these non-readers that they could do it too and showed them how. They played school with each other when they had free time before class. They listened to each other read and told each other words they didn't know. One by one, they struggled to understand. Many times during the year, a child would come to me, very surprised, and say, "Look, I can read!"

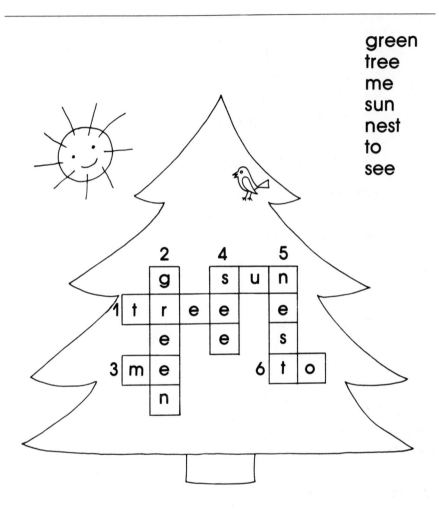

green
tree
me
sun
nest
to
see

Across →

1. This is a <u>tree</u>.

3. It looks pretty to <u>me</u>.

4. He likes to sit in the <u>sun</u>.

6. I want him <u>to</u> sing to me.

Down ↓

2. It is tall and <u>green</u>.

4. I can <u>see</u> a little bird in it.

5. Maybe he has a <u>nest</u> in the tree.

Figure 7-15   Crossword puzzle

This is a game.

1. Draw a cat.
2. Make a blue ball.
3. Put an X on the cat.
4. Add a hat to the cat.
5. Make some green grass.
6. Put a snake in the grass.
7. Put a yellow sun in the sky.
8. Make a tree next to the cat.
9. Put a nest in the tree.
10. Write your name.

Figure 7-16 Follow directions

Draw me.

I am yellow and hot.

I come out a lot.

I help you have fun.

You see, I'm the _____.

Figure 7-17 Draw the rhyme

You can do it too!

The principles that I followed throughout the year can be used in the home to achieve the same results. So let me summarize quickly what I did.

First, I set my goal to get every child reading. Everything I did contributed to that goal. Everything in the classroom taught another skill in reading.

Second, I provided a good model for the children to imitate. I read stories to them that I knew they would be able to read by themselves. I was patient and let each child develop at his own rate. I praised them all for whatever they were able to do.

Third, I presented reading as a puzzle that they were curious to do by themselves. I introduced it to them as a wonderful, special skill to master. I showed them that if you know how to read, you can have a lot of fun.

Fourth, I gave them the tools to be able to solve the puzzle. I taught them the symbols and the sounds that the symbols have. I taught them to recognize the common irregular words such as *the* and *one* that they would not be able to decode otherwise.

Fifth, I had them begin by learning the letters, then words, and then sentences. In teaching them words, I started with one- and two-letter words and then went on to two- and three-syllable words. I was always aware that the foundation for learning is built by going from the simple to the complex, the concrete to the abstract.

Last, I gave them many experiences with the same words so that, at the end of the year, they knew them without any doubts. They used the words every day. They wrote them, read them, said them, heard them. They gained a complete, total understanding of them.

You can achieve the same or better results with your child in your own home. When you decide that this is your goal, you will see the oppportunities for reading all around you. The learning will be natural and automatic for your child. Let me show you how to do it.

Chapter 8

How you can teach your child to read: Primary school years

I am a classic example of a parent who raises a non-reader. When I had my first child, Steve, I felt that the school should teach reading. When he wrote the letters, he made some of them backwards, and I didn't know what to do about it. I thought the school did. So I only answered the direct questions he asked, and I consciously tried not to teach him. I was afraid I would confuse him.

When he went into first grade, many in his class already knew how to read. He was placed in the middle group in a whole-word reading program. He read *was* for *saw* and *no* for *on*. He was irritable and angry because he didn't understand.

After a few months, the teacher sent home a list of words for me to teach him. When I began to see that this was my problem after all, I started to teach him to read at home.

From then on, I brought books home from the library that were on his reading level. Instead of a bedtime story, I listened to him read to me every night. Throughout his years in grade school, I added to his reading and writing skills at home.

By the end of the sixth grade, his achievement scores showed that he read at the twelfth-grade level. He scored in the 98 percentile on the entire battery of tests.

Teach your child at home and check on his learning throughout his school years to be sure he gains the skills in reading that he needs to succeed. I have listed the skills your child must master to begin to read fluently in figure 8-1. They don't develop in any

---

To learn to read, a child must be able to:

- name the letters of the alphabet, both in upper and lowercase
- associate one sound with each letter
- recognize some basic sight words
- see a connection between speech and print
- see a relationship between letters and words
- see a relationship between words and sentences
- know that you read from left to right, top to bottom

Figure 8-1 Beginning reading skills

regular, sequential order but are learned all at the same time. In other words, while your child is learning the names of the letters, he's also associating some of the sounds with them and beginning to notice that words are made up of letters that you read from the left side of the page to the right side. At the same time, he sees that you can say what you read, and he begins to remember some common words that he sees often.

When to begin

Actually, you began to teach your child to read when you set up a learning environment during his preschool years. When you talked and read to him every day, you taught him the meanings of the words that he's now almost ready to read.

No specific age indicates that a child's ready to read. But there are many signs that will tell you when to begin. As we've noted before, the child builds on previous knowledge. He needs to have visual and auditory discrimination, logical thinking ability, and a good understanding of language.

He tells you that he's ready to learn the letters of the alphabet when he notices geometric shapes in the everyday items around him. When he changes his round cookie into a square one with little bites and calls your attention to it, he gives you a message. When you cut his sandwich diagonally and he says, "Look, two triangles," he shows his visual awareness. When he sees a stop sign and identifies it by its shape alone, he also informs you of his progress.

The alphabet

When your child learns to recognize and name the letters of the alphabet, he takes the next step toward reading. However, before he can know the names of the letters, he needs to be familiar with their shapes. For this, he must see them often and note the differences in their outlines.

Alphabet blocks like those shown in figure 8-2 give your child good "hands-on" experiences. They let him sort the letters into groups. He'll turn the blocks so that he can put all the *A*'s together or so that he can spell his own name. You can ask him to give you an *A* or an *M*, and he can find it for you. Later, you can ask him to tell you the letter-name of a block.

Rubber alphabet puzzles like the ones in figure 8-3 let your child touch the outline of the letter as he replaces it in the board. They teach alphabetical order as they train his eye to observe the shape of each letter. (You can also get number puzzles like the one shown to teach the order and shapes of the numbers.)

Figure 8-2   Alphabet blocks

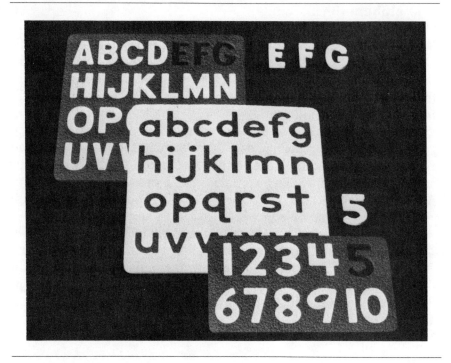

Figure 8-3   Rubber alphabet and number puzzles

A magnetic alphabet board with plastic letters is another tool for having your child touch the letters and learn their shapes. Fisher-Price makes the one shown in figure 8-4, with a spelling board on one side and a puzzle on the other. It comes with an upper-case, magnetic alphabet so your child can either match the letters to the printed ones in the trays on the puzzle side (the side shown in the figure) or make words on the spelling side.

As your child becomes familiar with the shapes of the letters, he'll become aware of them in other places. He'll begin to pay attention to them now in his alphabet picture books and coloring books. He'll begin to shape them out of clay.

Once your child recognizes the shapes of the letters, he needs to know their names. He accumulates this information from the experiences he has with letters. Slowly, he adds to his knowledge until he's memorized them all.

Make a letter chart with the alphabet in order, forming simple, easy-to-identify letters as shown in figure 8-5. Tell your child that

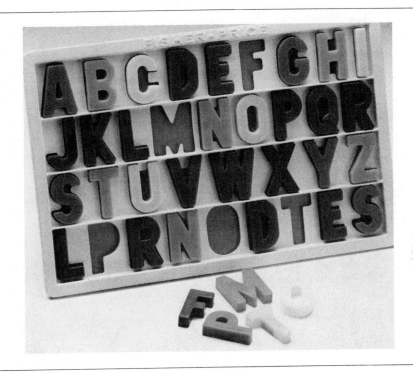

Figure 8-4   Magnetic alphabet board

there are 26 big letters and 26 small letters. Sing the alphabet song, and point to each letter as you name it. (If you don't already know this song, it's easy to learn. Simply sing the letters of the alphabet to the tune of "Twinkle, Twinkle, Little Star." End the song with "Now I know my ABC's, Won't you come and play with me.")

Some of the letters he'll learn very quickly. *A* is the first letter of the alphabet and looks like a triangle. *O* is a circle. *S* looks like a snake. *C* is a broken circle. *J* looks like a hook. *H* looks like a ladder.

Teach him to recognize the letters of his name. Make his name with alphabet blocks or any other letters that you have in your home. After he's seen his name a few times and recognizes it, tell him the names of the letters in it. He'll then begin to notice them on billboards and store signs. "There's my letter," he'll say.

Letters can be taught when he sees them on cereal boxes, food packages, street signs, calendars, etc. Always tell him the name of the letter when you have an opportunity. Gradually, he'll begin to recognize them and learn their names.

Figure 8-5 Upper and lowercase letters that are easy to read

Make or buy alphabet cards. On 4 x 6 cards, write the uppercase letters on one side and the lowercase letters on the other side:

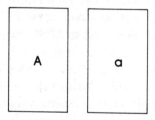

Eleven of the letters are the same in both sizes. These are *Cc*, *Kk*, *Oo*, *Pp*, *Ss*, *Uu*, *Vv*, *Ww*, *Xx*, *Yy*, *Zz*. *Jj*, *Hh*, *Tt*, *Mm*, and *Nn* are very similar. The remaining ten are the most difficult because they're different in upper and lowercase.

It's natural to confuse *b* with *d* and *p* with *q*. Don't be concerned or stress these letters more than the others. As your child sees them more and when they're part of words, his confusion will disappear.

If you want to follow Montessori's tactile approach, make sandpaper letters. Cut the letters from emery or sandpaper and paste them on 4 x 6 cards. Have your child touch them with his forefinger to learn the shape. If he touches them in the direction that he will print them, he lays the foundation for writing. Guide his finger from the top to the bottom of the letter the way he'll later write it with his pencil.

Your child will love to play with these alphabet cards. He'll try to find "his" letter. He'll want to know which one is "your" letter. His curiosity will provoke many questions about letters. Keep them in a specific place, like a shoebox, and treat them as something special.

Use these both for teaching and testing your child. Educators call them "flash" cards because when you show them to your child quickly, he should produce an automatic response to the visual stimulation. He must be able to look at the shape and identify it immediately by name.

To test your child's recognition, show him the cards in random order and ask him to name the letter that you show him. If he doesn't know it, smile, say the name of the letter, and go on to the next card. As you go through the stack, make two piles—one with those he knows and one with those he doesn't know. Children don't need to know *all* the letters before they learn to read words. But they should notice the different shapes of the letters. Your child has to make this distinction before he can assign a sound to each letter.

Each day thereafter, show him first the letters that he remembers to reinforce his acquired knowledge. Then say the others with him as you point to each one. He'll surprise you with how quickly he learns their names.

Next, print your child's name on a 4 x 6 card so he recognizes it by sight. Now when he scribbles and draws, he'll begin to try to write the first letter of his name, and then he'll want to learn to write his entire name.

Writing the letters like this is an integral part of learning to read because when a child forms the letters on paper, he imprints the shape in his mind. In other words, writing the letters helps him learn to identify them. It's not surprising, then, that more than half of the children in Dr. Durkin's studies learned to write before they learned to read. (Many began at age four.) And Montessori also concluded, "Writing precedes reading."

So encourage your child to learn the shapes of the letters by writing them. Wooden letters will teach the outlines as your child traces around them. Or you can make alphabet stencils for tracing from cardboard or sandpaper just as you cut out the geometric shapes earlier (see chapter 6).

A chalkboard will also help your child learn to write. Many have the letters printed at the top of the board. This gives a nearby example for the child to copy.

Another way to teach your child to write is to outline his name with dots on a piece of lined paper:

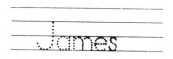

Here again, when he traces over the dots with his pencil, he learns the forms of the letters.

When you make the outlines, be sure to use both upper and lowercase letters. Very soon your child will be able to recognize his name any way that he sees it written. But when he gets to school, he'll be expected to write his name with a capital letter at the beginning and the rest in lowercase. Besides, he should become more familiar with the lowercase letter forms because they are used more often in reading.

Also, always write your child's name at the far left side of the paper to train his eyes to move from left to right in the direction of English print. This helps to avoid the problem of writing letters and words backwards. Repeated efforts establish the pattern of left-to-right progression.

The sounds of the letters

After your child develops an awareness of letters and recognizes his own name, he'll begin to notice words. Now is the time to show him that each letter stands for a sound. Since you've already taught him the names of most of the letters, you've prepared him to easily learn the sounds. Studies have shown that knowing the alphabet is the best single predictor of reading success in the early grades. This is because all but two of the letters of the alphabet have one major sound in their names.

To understand what I mean, say each letter of the alphabet aloud. As you pronounce its name, notice how you also say one major sound of the letter: *A* as in *apron*; *B* as in *bead*; *C* as in *ceiling*; *D* as in *deed*; *E* as in *me*; *F* as in *effort*; *G* as in *geography*; *H* as in *Rachel*; *I* as in *ice*; *J* as in *jay*; *K* as in *Kay*; *L* as in *bell*; *M* as in *Emily*; *N* as in *end*; *O* as in *oval*; *P* as in *Peter*; *R* as in *are*; *S* as in *Esther*; *T* as in *tea*; *U* as in *ukelele*; *V* as in *veto*; *X* as in *hex*; *Y* as in *why*; and *Z* as in *zebra*. Only *W* (stands for *wuh*) and *Q* (stands for *kwuh*) do not indicate the sounds that they represent. You can see that when your child has learned the letter-names, he's already mastered one sound for most of the letters (of course, some of the letters, like the vowels, have more than one major sound).

To teach the sounds, make or buy more elaborate alphabet cards, or modify the ones you already have. Once again, put both the upper and lowercase letter on the same card. Now, cut a picture from a magazine or draw one that represents the most common sound for that letter. Print the word for the picture on the bottom of the card. Choose words from figure 7-10 that are short and easy to read:

Some of the letters require special consideration as you make up these cards. First, for the vowels, teach only the short sound:

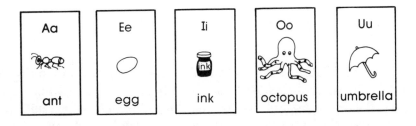

(Your child already knows the long sound, which is also the name of the letter.) And don't talk about long and short vowels. It only confuses children.

Second, few words begin with *X*. It's misleading to use a xylophone, for example, to stand for the sound of *X* because the beginning sound of *xylophone* is z-z-z. Tell your child that *X* is used at the end of words, such as *box, fox, ax,* and *wax*:

You want him to be able to "hear" the differences between the sounds and to associate one major sound for each letter.

Children should know right away why you want them to learn these letter-sounds. When they see the letter in the word, they begin to make the connection between speech and print. The picture helps them associate the object with the word; the word helps them associate the sound of the letter with the shape of the letter.

Your child will love to play with these cards. He'll learn as he looks at them again and again and talks to himself.

Later on, ask him to tell you what's on the cards. First point to the letter-name and then to the word for the object—*Aa, ant,* for example. Move your finger from left to right across the word to train his eye to move from left to right:

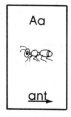

Richard Scarry's ABC Book will show your child many words that begin with each letter as it continues to enlarge his vocabulary. Point to the words as you say them. Again, this will help your child make the connection between the sounds he hears and the symbols he sees.

Now he'll begin to notice words everywhere you go. Encourage this by pointing out words on street and store signs, on food packages, and on games and toys. When you see the stop sign, tell him that the letter S has the sound of s-s-s. If he sees the sign "Men" on the restroom door and tells you, "That says 'boys,' " explain to him that M says m-m-m for men. Take the opportunities as they come along to slowly teach him this letter-sound correspondence.

Don't expect him to learn in a short time. Just keep providing him with information as he goes along. Help him when he shows an interest. Let him assimilate the knowledge at his own rate.

Now that he can recognize sounds and words as well as letters, he'll begin to write more and more. Montessori calls this "an explosion into writing." Provide him with many opportunities to write. Give him plenty of scratch paper, markers, crayons, and pencils.

The children in Dolores Durkin's studies seemed obsessed with writing. They copied pages from telephone books, words from calendars, and paragraphs from older siblings' workbooks. My first graders came in the morning and asked to be able to write. They wrote the same words again and again. They wrote the alphabet from A to Z. They wrote the numbers from 1 to 100. What seems repetitive to us is fun to children as they learn to read and write. This repetition creates automatic responses in reading, so you want to encourage it.

A sight vocabulary

As your child observes words in the world around him, he begins to remember a group of words that he recognizes on sight. He associates them with the places that he first sees them and then is surprised to find these words in other places.

For example, *stop* is a word that most children know because they see it often when they're out. With no conscious effort on my part, my son quickly learned *Exit, Standard, Dominick's, Men, Kellogg's, Hot Wheels*, etc. When he correctly identified a word, he was very pleased and asked about other words around him.

After I taught my first graders some of the most common words in reading, they pointed them out to me on bulletin boards as we walked through the halls in school. They recognized *for* in "For Sale" and quickly figured out the rest of the sign. They noticed *no, in,* and *the* in the sign "No smoking in the building" and correctly read it for me. When we went on a field trip, they were able to read signs that said "The Chicago Sun-Times" and "The Store for Big and Little Men."

Front	Back	Front	Back
a	A	blue	cue
I	I		due
is	Is		hue
			Sue
on	On	come	some
one	One	day	may
the	The		say
this	This		way
			play
to	To	go	no
two	Two		so
you	You	in	fin
all	ball		pin
	call		tin
	fall		win
	wall	it	bit
am	ham		fit
	Pam		hit
	ram		sit
	Sam	jump	bump
an	can		hump
	fan		dump
	man		lump
	pan	look	book
and	band		cook
	hand		took
	land		shook
	sand	me	be
as	has		he
at	cat		we
	hat		she
	fat	my	by
	mat		cry
big	dig		fly
	wig		try
	fig	not	cot
	pig		got
			hot
			pot

Figure 8-6   Group 1 sight words (part 1 of 2)

Front	Back	Front	Back
now	cow	see	free
	how		tree
	down		three
	brown		green
or	for	up	cup
			pup
red	bed		
	fed	will	bill
	led		fill
	Ted		mill
			sill
run	fun		
	bun		
	sun		
	gun		

Figure 8-6   Group 1 sight words (part 2 of 2)

When your child shows an interest in words, teach him some of the most commonly-used words in reading. Begin with the group 1 sight words in figure 8-6. Use them to make up 4 x 6 word cards for your child.

The words in the list fall into two groups, depending on what type of word cards you should make. For the first ten I've listed, print the word in all lowercase letters on one side of the card. On the other side, print the same word but begin it with a capital letter. This will enable your child to recognize the word when it's at the beginning of a sentence and when it's in the middle of a sentence. Examples are: a—A; is—Is; the—The; this—This; and you—You.

The rest of the words will serve two purposes. First, they'll show that letters in combination make words. You'll print these words on the front sides of the cards. Examples are an, and, as, and at. Second, they'll show later on that when one or two letters are placed before the word or when the first letter of the word is changed, a new word is formed. These are the words you'll print on the back side of the cards. Examples are cat, hat, fat, and mat on the back of the at card.

When you begin, show your child all the cards on the front side only. You may be surprised to find that he already knows or can sound out many of them. (This is what Dolores Durkin found when she tested incoming first graders.)

Say the word slowly as you move your finger from left to right across the card so your child can associate the sound of each letter with the symbol:

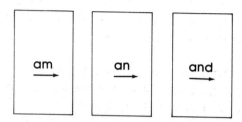

As I've said before, this trains your child's eye to move from left to right and indicates that the first letter is the first sound of the word.

Some of the words in the list, though, are irregular in their letter-sound relationships. They can't be sounded out, so basically you'll teach them as "whole words." Examples are *one*, *the*, *two*, *you*, and *come*. Merely tell your child that these are unusual words and must be remembered because they are special. He won't think this is difficult to learn if you present it in this way.

Also, when you teach the word *a*, assign the sound of *uh* to it, as in the sentence "I have a ball." This is the dictionary pronunciation for this small article, and it's also the third sound for the letter *a*. (The others are long *a* as in *acorn* and short *a* as in *apple*.) The *uh* sound will be used later in *away*, *again*, *about*, and *around*.

Is and *this* illustrate the two different sounds of *s* at the end of words. Sometimes, *s* has the sound of *z*. Examples are *is* and *as*. Sometimes *s* has a hissing sound, as in *this*. Point these differences out to your child when you show him the word cards. You'll find that he accepts these irregularities with no apparent extra interest or confusion. If you introduce him to these differences gradually, he'll add them to his knowledge easily and naturally.

After you say the words with your child a few times, test his recognition. Show him a word card and wait for him to say the word. If he can't do it right away, repeat the teaching procedure. Say the word slowly as you move your finger from left to right across the card.

Make two piles of words as you show him the cards. In one group, put the words that he recognizes and "knows." In the other group, put those that he's unable to say without help. When you've gone through all the word cards, you can count the ones he knows to give him (and you) the satisfaction of progress. You'll be surprised to see how quickly your child learns to recognize these words. (This is one reason why the "whole-word" or "look-say" method is so popular. But we aren't really teaching sight recognition. We're clearly showing a letter-sound correspondence whenever one exists.)

Let him have these word cards to play with just as he examined the letter cards when he was learning to recognize the letters. He'll probably put cards together to make sentences. Show him some of these possibilities if he doesn't do it by himself. This gives him the understanding that a word is a group of letters that means something special and that a sentence is a group of words that tells something.

Try some of the following combinations with him:

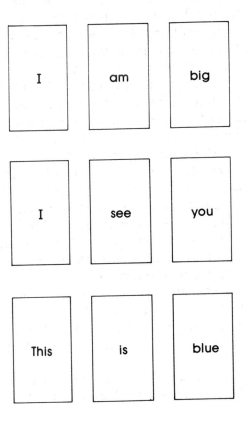

Use the word card with his name on it to create sentences such as the following:

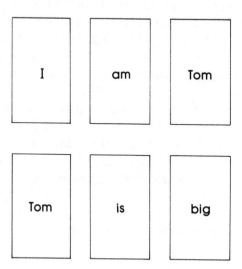

Now your child will start to write these words on his chalkboard and on the scratch paper you've given him. He'll practice the same thing again and again.

Write notes to him. To children, reading is a wonderful game or puzzle. It's like a secret code. They love to be able to figure out words. Try "You will go to the *zoo*" or "You and I will see a *zebra*." It's fun to add a new word now and then—not to teach it as a sight word but to arouse your child's curiosity. Often he's able to sound out this new word on his own.

After he's mastered all the words on the front of the cards in group 1, he's ready to learn new skills. Show him the front side of each card and then turn it over. See if he can read the words on the back sides of the cards. Many children see the rhyming relationships and word patterns immediately. But if your child doesn't, don't be disappointed because he'll learn easily.

As an example, let's use the *at* card:

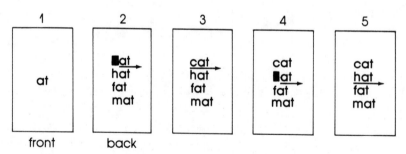

Show him the front side of the card. He'll say "at." Then turn the card over. Cover up the *c* and he'll recognize the word he sees and say "at." Now, ask your child, "What sound does the letter *c* have?" After he tells you the sound, uncover the *c* and say, "Put a *c* in front of *at* and you have," pause, "*cat*." Again, say each word slowly as you move your finger underneath it from left to right across the card. Repeat this procedure for *hat, fat,* and *mat.*

Let him assimilate this new knowledge slowly. Don't try to teach him more than one new word pattern at a time. Of course, if he sees the relationship right away and wants to try other word patterns, go ahead. You're the teacher; you evaluate your child's progress!

Sometimes two consonants together make one sound, such as *sh* and *th.* In group 1, you'll teach the sound of *th* in *the, this,* and *three. Sh* is in the words *she* and *shook.* Call his attention to the way the mouth moves to form these sounds. This will help him remember the differences.

Sometimes, two consonants each have their own sound at the beginning or end of the word. Examples from group 1 are *fly, cry, try, play, free, tree, green, brown,* and *blue.* If you enunciate clearly as you say these words slowly, your child will be able to hear the sounds of both consonants. In this way, you reinforce his association of the sounds of the letters with the sight of the letters.

Each word card, then, teaches more than one skill. For example, with *see,* you first teach your child the sound of two *e*'s together. Then, on the back, he learns consonant combinations. To teach these, take one consonant at a time:

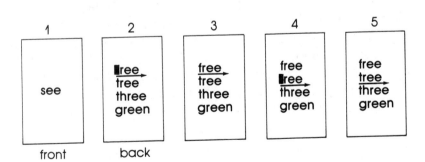

In other words, on the back of the *see* card, cover up the *f* in *free* with your finger. Ask, "What sound does *r* have?" After your child tells you, say, "That's right. *R-r-r* plus *ee* says *ree.*" As before, move your finger from left to right underneath the word as you slowly say it. Then, move your finger to uncover the *f.* Now ask, "What sound

Front	Back	Front	Back
after	After	find	bind
are	Are		mind
			kind
good	Good		blind
his	His	five	dive
said	Said		hive
			live
they	They		strive
who	Who	four	pour
ate	mate	get	let
	gate		bet
	plate		set
	skate		wet
black	back	her	Bert
	Jack		pert
	sack		perk
	tack		jerk
but	cut	here	where
	hut		there
	jut	him	dim
	nut		Jim
came	same		rim
	tame		Tim
	fame		
	flame	little	brittle
			whittle
car	bar		middle
	far		fiddle
	mar		
	tar	must	dust
did	bid		rust
	hid		gust
	kid		just
	lid		
		new	flew
eat	meat		stew
	neat		crew
	seat		brew
	treat		

Figure 8-7 Group 2 sight words (part 1 of 2)

Front	Back	Front	Back
old	cold	ten	hen
	bold		pen
	told		then
	mold		when
out	pout	too	loon
	spout		moon
	shout		soon
	about		spoon
saw	law	what	that
	raw	yellow	bellow
	paw		fellow
	draw		mellow

Figure 8-7   Group 2 sight words (part 2 of 2)

does *f* have?" After your child tells you, say, "That's right. And if you put an *f* in front of *ree* you have *free*."

Once again, as the teacher, you go from the part to the whole; from the simple to the complex. You break the word into parts and then go to the whole word. Always speak slowly so your child can hear the different sounds easily. Follow the same procedure for the other words on the card. In this way, you train his eye to see the differences and his ear to hear the differences. You also show him that reading is logical.

When you're sure that he understands these consonant combinations (and he'll learn fast), just show him the front and back of each card and have him read the words to you.

Additional word patterns and sight words

After your child has learned the words in the group 1 list, he'll begin to read more of the printed material in the world around him. But to be sure that he gains the necessary skills to become a fluent reader, I have included group 2 and group 3 word lists (figures 8-7 and 8-8). Each set of words introduces new word patterns and irregular words that he must know to be able to decode all the combinations that compose the English language.

Front	Back	Front	Back
again	Again	going	coming
any	Any		giving
eight	Eight		liking
every	Every		taking
have	Have	hurt	Burt
laugh	Laugh		burn
of	Of		turn
once	Once		churn
over	Over	know	low
please	Please		flow
put	Put		blow
seven	Seven		grow
six	Six	light	might
under	Under		night
want	Want		right
were	Were		sight
with	With	like	bike
write	Write		hike
yes	Yes		Mike
could	would		strike
	should	pretty	Betty
first	dirt		jetty
	firm	ride	hide
	shirt		side
	skirt		bride
give	live		pride
goes	foes	stop	hop
	hoes		mop
	toes		pop
	woes		flop
		take	bake
			cake
			make
			wake

Figure 8-8 Group 3 sight words (part 1 of 2)

Front	Back	Front	Back
them	hem	walk	balk
	gem		talk
	stem		stalk
	tempt		chalk

Figure 8-8   Group 3 sight words (part 2 of 2)

Begin to add words in your notes to him from the group 2 list:

I will go in a *little* bit.

See if he can sound them out. With the word *little*, for example, see if he can break the word into parts and figure the ending out for himself. If he can't, cover up the *tle* to train his eye to separate words into known parts. Then uncover it after he reads *lit* so he can add *tle*.

On the back of the *little* card are *brittle* and *whittle* to illustrate other words with this pattern. Then, to show that more words have double consonants and the *le* ending, *middle* and *fiddle* are also on the back of the same card.

Here's another sentence you could use in your notes:

You can go *too.*

Too is easy to learn because your child knows *to* from group 1. *Too* introduces the *oo* sound of two *o*'s together as in *soon* and *moon*. (He already knows the sound of two *o*'s in *look* and *book*.)

Writing notes is the best way to show that reading is meaningful. Notes show a direct relationship between talk and reading. Besides, children are highly motivated to try to find out what they say.

In group 2, you will also teach the irregular words *are, said,* and *they*. Be sure to tell your child these words are special and must be remembered even though the spelling doesn't make too much sense. In this way, you train his eye to look at the individual letters carefully and to remember the unusual words.

What and *that* are spelled alike at the end but sound different. With *what*, you also teach the sound of the two consonants *wh*.

Likewise, *here* doesn't sound the same as *where* and *there*, but they all have the same spelling at the end. Show your child the *here* in *where* and *there*. Say, "If you put a *t* in front of *here*, you have there. If you put a *w* in front of *here*, you have *where*." Then call his attention to the *th* and *wh* combinations of letters that make new sounds.

In group 2, you also teach *came* and *ate*, which have silent *e*'s at the end. Don't make too much of this. You taught *come* in group 1. Use *came* to train your child's eye to notice the difference in the middle of the word. Just introduce the *ate* word pattern as naturally as any other. In group 3, you will have *ake* in *take, bake, cake, make,* and *wake*. Slowly, a pattern for words with *e* at the end will be established in your child's mind.

With the second group of words, your child will also learn the *er* sound in *her* and *after*. Other common letter combinations that you'll teach are *aw* in *saw*, *ea* in *eat*, *ew* in *new*, and *ind* in *find*. And you'll train your child's eye to notice some double consonant endings: *ck* in *black*; *st* in *must*; and *ld* in *old*.

Group 3 introduces the irregular word *laugh*, which makes most children laugh, and they don't forget it. *Have* and *were* are two words with an *e* at the end that don't follow any rule. *Again* and *put* are two more words that simply must be remembered.

Pretty changes to *pritty* when we say it. Try to pronounce the *e* as in *egg* and explain that when we speak fast, we change the sound of the word, but the spelling will always be the same.

In this way, you give your beginning reader a regular guideline he can follow. When you teach him to recognize the vowels as true sounds—*a* as in *ant*, *e* as in *egg*, *i* as in *ink*, *o* as in *otter*, *u* as in *up*—especially in the middle of words, you train him to hear the differences that help him spell correctly. You don't have to worry that this will cause him to misread words; I've found, instead, that it helps children figure out new words. And with practice, he'll learn all the irregularities and memorize them so that he always pronounces the words properly when he's reading aloud. Just remember, he can't learn everything at once.

Under and *seven* are two-syllable words that train the child's eye to see the parts in longer words. *Every* is a three-syllable word with a *y* ending. *Know* exemplifies silent *k* and the *ow* sound; *eight* and *light* illustrate silent *gh*; *walk* has silent *l*; and *write* has silent *w*. Merely point these patterns out to your child in a matter-of-fact manner. You'll find that he accepts this new information with no difficulty at all.

The verb ending *ing* is another important addition to your child's knowledge. He'll probably be able to sound out *going*. If he can't, cover up the *ing* on the card so that he sees the parts of the word. On the back of the card are *coming, giving, liking,* and *taking*, which drop the final e before adding *ing*. So this card will also introduce him to words that have this form.

With the words in these three groups, your child learns the most common irregularities and the most common regular word patterns. Figure 8-9 gives a more complete list that represents the 220 most often-used words in the English language (it's the same as the list in figure 7-6 and includes most of the words in the three groups that I have selected as most important for beginning readers). If your child knows these words, he'll be able to read on the third-grade level. After your child has been reading for several months, check his ability to read the entire list. It will give you information about how well he can read new material.

Read, read, read

To master both regular and irregular word patterns, your child must read regularly and often. When he reads, he practices the skills he has learned. He reinforces his memory of the irregular sight words that cannot be sounded out. And he improves his ability to decode new words because he uses his memory of word patterns to figure out the new words in his books. When he reads, his success motivates him to want to read more. This is the cycle of learning.

After you begin to teach your child letters and sounds and words, continue to read to him every day. As he learns to sound out and recognize words, he'll ask about the words he sees in the books you read. He'll pretend that he can read and will want to "read" a familiar story to you. In this way, he starts to read on his own.

Use *Richard Scarry's Best Word Book Ever* to teach him to sound out longer words. You can use it to show him the patterns in words. The pictures give him clues and build his confidence in his ability to read. When he was younger, he learned new words to describe objects in his environment from this book. Now, he learns to read those words.

Any reading material that is available will teach your child to read. But two books that guarantee success easily are *Go, Dog, Go* by P. D. Eastman and *Put Me In The Zoo* by Robert Lopshire. (Both are from the Beginner Books Series by Random House, Inc.) Children want to read these books because they love the pictures and the endearing stories. Both use the child's knowledge of colors and rhyme to teach words.

Pre-primer

a	find	is	not	three
and	for	it	one	to
away	funny	jump	play	two
big	go	little	red	up
blue	help	look	run	we
can	here	make	said	where
come	I	me	see	yellow
down	in	my	the	you

Primer

all	do	no	she	well
am	eat	now	so	went
are	four	on	soon	what
at	get	our	that	white
ate	good	out	there	who
be	have	please	they	will
black	he	pretty	this	with
brown	into	ran	too	yes
but	like	ride	under	
came	must	saw	want	
did	new	say	was	

First grade

after	fly	how	open	then
again	from	just	over	there
an	give	know	put	think
any	going	let	round	walk
as	had	live	some	when
ask	has	may	stop	
by	her	of	take	
could	him	old	thank	
every	his	once	them	

Figure 8-9 Dolch basic word list (part 1 of 2)

Second grade

always	does	made	tell	why
around	don't	many	their	wish
because	fast	off	these	work
been	first	or	those	would
before	five	pull	upon	write
best	found	read	us	your
both	gave	right	use	
buy	goes	sing	very	
call	green	sit	wash	
cold	its	sleep	which	

Third grade

about	eight	if	only	ten
better	fall	keep	own	today
bring	far	kind	pick	together
carry	full	laugh	seven	try
clean	got	light	shall	warm
cut	grow	long	show	
done	hold	much	six	
draw	hot	myself	small	
drink	hurt	never	start	

Figure 8-9   Dolch basic word list (part 2 of 2)

The pictures give clues so that your child "can do it by himself." He'll learn to read these books because there are only one or two words on each page. The words are frequently repeated, and he'll begin to recognize the most common ones. He'll learn a basic sight vocabulary and add to it as he reads the succeeding pages that have more words on them. He'll want to read these books again and again until he's completely mastered them.

When your child starts to "read" to you, have him put his finger on each word as he says it. This will make him look at each word individually. It will also train his eye to move from left to right across the page. Your child must learn to look carefully at each word to correctly sound it out. He must also know that each word begins with the letters on the left. He'll stop touching each word with his finger when he no longer needs to do this to keep his eye on each set of symbols. (And some children skip this stage entirely.)

At first, he'll read everything aloud. In this way, he makes a direct connection between speech and print. When he hears the words in meaningful text, he knows that he's correctly decoded the letters. Later, when he's sure of his knowledge, he'll read silently to himself. For now, though, he needs feedback that he's drawing the right conclusions.

You reinforce his success when you listen to him read aloud and smile your approval of his accurate decoding. You prevent his future errors when you simply give him letter-and-sound skills if he makes a mistake. Don't let him develop the habit of guessing. Always show him that the letters have sounds that tell him the word.

Thus, *dog* cannot be *puppy* because *d* says *d-d-d*. If he reads *eat* as *at*, point out that *e* and *a* together say *e-e*. Show him that he must always pay close attention to each symbol on the page. Provide him with phonetic tools so he can sound out words by himself.

Practice makes perfect!

I frequently told my first graders, "I want you to know this well enough so that you can read backwards, forwards, and upside down." I'll always remember one little girl who chuckled and beamed and said, "I can't wait 'til we get to the upside-down part!"

But, it's true! For reading to be pleasurable, the responses to the visual symbols must be automatic. For this to happen, your child needs to use these skills every day. He needs to read and to write to make this knowledge "part and parcel" of him. At the end of the year, my first graders could read the most common words any way that they were printed. They could do this because they had learned to recognize these words in many different places.

The letter-and-sound code fascinates children. They soon see the relationship between reading and writing. They love to read all the words they see. And they love to write words they have never seen. In the earliest stages of learning, they need to know that they can. If they have opportunities to read and write with success, they gain the confidence to continue to accumulate the skills they need to become mature readers.

So give your child writing exercises to be sure he remembers and understands what you're teaching him. When he begins to learn the names of the letters, give him specific letters to print on his scratch paper or chalkboard. For example, ask him to write the letter *E* for you. Your child will progress from being able to select the letter that you name from a group of letters to being able to write the letter that stands for a sound. For example, ask him to write the letter that says *p-p*.

After he has mastered the letter-and-sound correspondences, dictate words to him that have a regular word pattern. For example, begin with *an*. Then, ask him to write *man, can, pan, tan, ran,* and *fan*. Do this same exercise with the other common words in group 1, such as *and, at, in, it,* etc.

When he's confident with these word patterns and says, "That's easy," mix them up. For example, direct him to write *cat, mat, man, pan, ran, run, sun, fun*. As he writes, he must think of the differences between the words.

Help him have success. Let him know that he can do it. Say each word slowly. Pronounce each sound distinctly. Give him clues if he looks puzzled. Ask him, "What letter says *t-t*? What letter says *n-n*?" If he can't answer, you know that his understanding isn't complete, and he needs more drill with the word flash cards.

After he can write the regular words and sees how words are formed, dictate sentences to him. Begin with simple ones, such as "I can go" or "I am _____ (your child's name)." Show him how to space the words and tell him to put a period at the end of the sentence. In this way, he begins to understand punctuation and word order.

As he progresses, make your sentences longer. Dictate some irregular words so he can learn how to spell these too.

When he makes a mistake, show him the right way to do it. Gradually, with practice, he'll accumulate the beginning skills if he's permitted to "try, try again." His curiosity and his need for repetition will provide the motivation he needs to persevere.

But writing is only half of the communication process. Fluency in reading results from wide reading.

To increase his skills, your child should read at least half an hour a day at home. Daily repetition assures the continual development of vocabulary and word-pattern recognition.

Read together. Don't stop because he has begun to read to himself. When he reads to you, he gets the individual help he needs. You answer his specific questions about reading. You fill in the gaps of his knowledge.

After he can read the beginning books you have at home, take him to the library to introduce him to the vast amount of literature he can now explore. In the children's section, books are color-coded to indicate levels of difficulty. Guide your child to those marked "easiest" to give him many opportunities to practice the beginning skills you've taught him. In addition to the fiction that's available, Harper and Row publishes an I Can Read series that has a wide variety of interesting and easy sport, science, and mystery books.

Let your child repeat the same words in his books and writing. Don't push him to read three- and four-syllable words. (Help him to break them into parts when he does come across them, however.) Don't ask him to decode lots of words that he doesn't understand. (Tell him the meanings of words he doesn't know as he encounters them, however.) Don't require him to read longer sentences or smaller print or more involved stories. And don't insist that he read faster. Let him have continued success with the skills he has now.

As your child progresses, he'll select more difficult books to read. Guide him from the beginning fiction books to other sections of the children's room in the library.

Children's Press has produced a slightly more difficult non-fiction series—The True Book of Horses, Dinosaurs, Health, Communication, Transportation, etc. G. P. Putnam's Sons has See and Read biographies of the presidents. Thomas Y. Crowell Company presents the life stories of famous Americans such as Jim Thorpe, Maria Tallchief, Cesar Chavez, and Malcolm X. Math is represented by Franklin Watts, Inc. with its Let's Find Out About Addition, Subtraction, Fractions, etc. A great variety of primary-level books will give your child the message that reading can be an absorbing activity.

Gradually, he'll enlarge his speaking and reading vocabulary as he reads more. Gradually, he'll add irregular word patterns to his memory. Gradually, he'll note changes in verb tenses, plurals, compound words, possessives, contractions—all the variations of English grammar that create interesting reading material.

Right now, he needs to know that he can read and write. Right now, he needs to see that reading is fun and that he can use the skills every day to communicate with others. Right now, he needs to develop the positive feelings about reading that will guarantee his success in school.

Chapter 9

How you can raise your child's reading level in 6 weeks: Grades 3-5

When my second child, Jennifer, started first grade, she had already begun to read. It was to be expected. After all, I'd established a learning environment in the home. I'd answered her questions. I'd made sure she knew the alphabet and most sounds for the letters. I'd taught her some sight words, and one day I realized that she'd begun to read.

Jennifer loved school and had success in every subject. I was very busy in my own work and felt confident that she had a good start. Now the rest was up to the school. Conferences with her teachers in the first two grades indicated satisfactory progress. In fact, she made excellent progress in vocabulary development and reading comprehension. After awhile, I neither read to her every day nor listened to her read to me every day. I assumed she would continue to achieve.

At the end of the third grade, her achievement scores indicated a reading level of 3.5 (third year, fifth month), and that's better than average. For the entire battery of tests, she scored "high average." I didn't see a problem.

But I did observe that her cursive writing wasn't as good as her printing. And I became aware that when she wrote notes to me, she didn't spell words correctly or punctuate properly. Also, it seemed to me that the books she read weren't very difficult. In fact, she didn't seem to read as much anymore. The signs of trouble were present, but I didn't heed them.

To be an accomplished reader, a child must be able to:

- break words into syllables
- recognize long and short vowel sounds in words
- recognize vowel combinations
- recognize vowel-and-consonant combinations
- identify spelling patterns and rules
- understand that a period means to stop and a comma means to pause or take a breath
- read from left to right across the line without jumping around on the page

Figure 9-1 Advanced reading skills

At the fourth-grade conference, her teacher told me that Jennifer "needed to improve." (Our school doesn't give grades until the sixth year.) The report said that Jennifer didn't pay attention in class; she didn't finish her workbook; she didn't do any extra projects. Her papers were messy; her attitude was negative; she didn't seem to care what kind of work she did in school.

I wasn't too surprised because I had some of the same problems with her at home. I had attributed these behaviors to her easygoing, pleasant personality. Now, I began to look at her messy room and non-caring attitude as indicators of a total situation. However, I still failed to give her skills. I didn't really know where to begin.

Jennifer's achievement scores at the end of the fourth grade gave me the answers. While her reading score had increased to 4.5 (fourth year, fifth month), she had dropped to "average" in the entire battery of tests. Significantly, the greatest decreases were in vocabulary, spelling, and reading comprehension. Now, I knew what to do.

I checked her reading mastery on my own informal test and discovered that she lacked some of the important skills listed in figure 9-1. Failure to acquire these skills had resulted in bad habits that interfered with her ability to understand what she read. This inability had reduced her pleasure in reading, affected her achievement in other subjects, and caused her negative attitude toward school. I had to help her reverse this cycle of failure.

I developed a program that taught her letter-and-sound correspondences to improve her spelling and reading. As she read *correctly* every day and understood what she read, her vocabulary began to expand. After six weeks of my summer instruction, she returned to school. When she was tested for placement in reading groups, she was astounded. She had skipped a level.

Immediately, her attitude toward her work changed to a positive determination to do well. She now finished her work because she could read the directions and understand what she was supposed to do.

This time I didn't stop there. I continued a regular program. We read together almost every night—the equivalent of two hours a week.

Her progress continued. But it was slow and had its setbacks. After six weeks in the new reading group, her teacher called to say that Jennifer had been misplaced. The options were to put Jennifer back in her old group or to keep her in her present group with a volunteer tutor. I insisted on the latter alternative and didn't worry because I knew she would continue to advance her skills as I worked with her at home.

No volunteer tutor could be found right away, but it didn't matter; two months later, Jennifer had successfully made the transition. Her daily scores were above the critical mark and steadily became better. Six months after I began the remediation, she could read on the sixth-grade level.

Now, she began to ask her teachers if she could do extra reports. She took pride in her work and every day could chart evidence of some success. Either it was a perfect score on a spelling test or a high mark on a social studies test or a positive comment on a book report. Now that she knew how to read accurately, all her schoolwork improved.

You can use this reading program to teach your primary-grade child to read better before he develops any problems in school. Or you can use it to remediate an older child who has never mastered the fundamental word patterns that he needs to be able to read on the sixth-grade level and beyond.

The steps to follow are simple. First, find out how well your child reads. Second, set a regular time to read with your child. Third, use the word cards in this chapter to teach word patterns. Fourth, help your child with specific problems as you listen to him read to you.

Find out your child's reading level

There are two ways to evaluate your child's reading progress. First, ask his teacher to share his reading scores with you. This will tell you if he's performing on grade level. Then, do your own evaluation when you listen to your child read to you. This will tell you his specific problems with reading.

In our schools, several nationally standardized reading tests are given to all the pupils. These show how well the children in your school have mastered skills in comparison with all the children in the country. Three tests that are used most often are the Iowa Test of Basic Skills, The Gates-Mikillop Reading Diagnostic Test, and the Stanford Achievement Test. Results from any of these standardized tests will show you the strengths and weaknesses of your child in reading.

Even if these tests indicate performance on grade level, do your own evaluation. First, have your child read *aloud* a page from a book that he is currently reading. It can be a school text or a fiction book—even a magazine. You want to hear him read something on his level. You hope he'll be able to read this passage smoothly and comfortably. He should stop when he sees a period and pause when he sees a comma. He should be able to read this material with the natural expression and phrasing that the text stimulates. If he doesn't, you already have indicators of his reading ability.

Next, have him read something above his level. When he reads material that frustrates him, he'll show you how he tries to figure out words. Whether he's in the third grade and shows normal progress or whether he's in a higher grade and has known problems, see how well he can read the newspaper. The newspaper is written between the seventh- and the eleventh-grade level of readability. We know that it will frustrate him.

Have him read *aloud* a feature article, nationally syndicated column, or the sports page. Here, the material will be interesting, and he'll want to read it for you. Although the vocabulary may be less familiar to your child, the sentence structure will be fairly simple. Even a beginning reader can read some of the words.

Your child will have to rely on his understanding of the letter-and-sound correspondences to read at this level. Unless he's an advanced reader, however, he won't know the meanings of all the words that he correctly decodes. This is to be expected. But as he tries to make sense of this material, he'll show you how he solves the problem of reading unknown words.

He may substitute words he knows for the ones that are in the newspaper that he doesn't know. He may omit words and add his own to get meaning. If he's only learned to recognize whole words, he won't be able to sound out the three- and four-syllable words in the article. How he reads this material will tell you what problems he has in reading.

Make a list of the words that cause him to stumble. If they're all long words, it indicates that he doesn't see the separate parts of a word. If he adds, omits, or substitutes words, he's learned to guess rather than to use skills. If he reads a few words from one line of type and then a few words from another line of type, if he loses his place often, or if he repeats the same words, his eyes don't move from word to word across the page. In all instances, he needs drill in letter-and-sound correspondences.

At this time, then, note all the behaviors that your child displays as he reads. These are the indicators of his reading problem. Later, their disappearance will mark his progress.

I was shocked to hear Jennifer read the newspaper and, again, *Sports Illustrated*. She exhibited all the signs of a poor reader that I have listed above. If I hadn't been a teacher, I would have insisted that she go to a reading clinic. Instead, I decided to help her myself. It turned out to be a great experience for both of us.

Set aside a regular time

As a working parent, I know how hard it is to find time and energy to teach your child. But to make this reading program work, you must set aside one half hour a day four times a week. Your child will improve in six weeks only if he practices regularly. This is the most important factor in the formula for reading success.

As we've noted many times, repetition is a key learning tool. The child learns by doing the same thing again and again. If your child has been reading poorly for many years, he's been doing the same wrong thing again and again. Now, he needs to regularly repeat the right skills to establish the proper patterns to read accurately.

When you set a definite time to read together, you establish the reading habit. For Jennifer and me, the best time was at the end of the day as part of our bedtime ritual. In our household after dinner, the phone stops ringing and a quiet period begins. I don't go out much on weekday evenings, so this was the natural time to use for reading.

When we began the reading program, though, even this time always seemed wrong. So I tried other times of the day that didn't work as well for me because I wanted to make the lessons pleasant for Jennifer. Still I had the same results. I finally set the time that was best for me—after all, I was the teacher.

Jennifer clearly did not want to read. She always gave an excuse. Either she complained that she was too tired because she'd read a lot in school that day, or she insisted that now her favorite program came on television. Always, she begged, "Not now." Always, she began the lesson with a negative attitude.

This was a conflict I had only as a parent. Other children that I taught came to me willingly and gladly and were grateful for my help. Jennifer's teacher even suggested that if I taught my own child, I would set up a learning problem. Since Jennifer already had a learning problem, I decided to ignore her reluctance to read with me and began the lessons.

However, if I hadn't put the four half-hour time periods into my weekly schedule, I would have given up the struggle. As the scheduled hour neared for each lesson, I prepared myself for Jennifer's negative behavior. Firmly, and sometimes heatedly, I insisted that *now* was our time to read. When she saw there was no way out of it, she stopped resisting and accepted the reading routine. (After her reading improved and the habit had been established, she asked to read with me.)

Use the word-pattern cards

The plan for the reading program is simple. You'll make flash cards to teach the letter-and-sound patterns that form words. Part of each period will be spent teaching these word patterns, and the remainder of the time will be spent reading.

You'll need 100 plain 4 x 6 or 3 x 5 cards. With a marker, print the letters that stand for a sound pattern on the front of each card. On the back, print the words that illustrate these sound patterns. The sound patterns and words you should use are shown in figure 9-2.

The first week, you'll spend more than half of the allotted time showing your child the cards. Each day the amount of time spent on the cards will lessen as your child quickly learns the patterns. Each day he'll incorporate these word patterns into his reading.

Beginning Consonant Combinations*

Front	Back	Front	Back
br	ring	scr	rub
	bring		scrub
	brim		scrap
	brisk		scratch
ch	chill	sh	shin
	chin		shut
	check		ship
	chunk		show
cr	rash	shr	shrimp
	crash		shrink
	crack		shrivel
	crush		shrill
dr	rip	spr	ring
	drip		spring
	drill		sprinkle
	drop		sprightly
fr	red	str	ring
	Fred		string
	fresh		street
	frog		strike
gr	rip	th	the
	grip		then
	grab		this
	grow		that
pr	ray	thr	rush
	pray		thrush
	press		thrash
	print		thrown
			thrill
sc	can		
	scan		
	scour		
	scoop		

*   Note that the first word on the back often drops one or more of the beginning consonants. When we take words apart like this, we train the child to look at the letters more carefully and notice how words are built of parts he already knows.

Figure 9-2   Word–pattern cards (part 1 of 7)

Beginning Consonant Combinations (continued)

Front	Back	Front	Back
tr	trip	wh	what
	trap		when
	trot		where
	truck		who
	trick		why

Consonant Combinations

gh as f	rough	ph as f	phone
	tough		phrase
	enough		pharmacy
	cough		autograph
	laugh		pamphlet

Endings

ance	importance	dgy	fudgy
	resistance		pudgy
	attendance		smudgy
	ignorance		stodgy
ce	face	ed	shouted
	pace		decided
	place		hitched
	prince		crawled
ck	deck	ence	influence
	duck		providence
	pick		confidence
	pack		residence
cy	Nancy		preference
	fancy	er	better
	lacy		butter
	Tracy		ladder
dge	ledge		upper
	sledge	gy	bulgy
	hedge		dingy
	wedge		stingy
			strategy

Figure 9-2   Word–pattern cards (part 2 of 7)

Endings (continued)

Front	Back	Front	Back
ia	Asia	nks	winks
	Malaysia		drinks
	aphasia		sinks
	malaria		blinks
	Australia	tch	crutch
ing	whipping		scratch
	fading		ditch
	topping		witch
	aping	y	by
	raving		my
ive	active		rely
	captive		deny
	detective		
	attentive	y to ier	happy–
	passive		happier
le	little		funny–
	rattle		funnier
	hobble		
	bottle	y to ies	candy–
ngs	hangs		candies
	lungs		
	bangs		fairy–
	swings		fairies
nk	sink		
	drink		
	rank		
	drank		

Vowel Combinations

Front	Back	Front	Back
ai	aim	au	haul
	mail		Paul
	pain		fraud
	quaint		fault

Figure 9-2 Word–pattern cards (part 3 of 7)

Vowel Combinations (continued)

Front	Back	Front	Back
ea	head	oo	book
	bread		look
	wealth		cook
	feather		poor
ea	eat	oo	moon
	seat		spoon
	meal		croon
	beak		swoon
	speak	ou	out
ee	eel		trout
	peel		flour
	deer		found
	eerie	ou	young
ei	eight		famous
	weigh		enormous
	neighbor		nervous
ie	pie		marvelous
	die	ue	cue
	dried		blue
	spied		flue
ie	field		true
	wield	ui	suit
	piece		fruit
	grief		juice
oa	goat		fruitful
	coast		juicy
	load		
	groan		
oe	hoe		
	toe		
	foe		
	doe		
oi	oil		
	oink		
	point		
	soil		

Figure 9-2 Word–pattern cards (part 4 of 7)

Vowel and Consonant Combinations

Front	Back	Front	Back
air	hair	come	comely
	fair		comeback
	lair		welcome
	chair		income
			become
alk	talk		
	walk	dgi	grudging
	balk		judging
	chalk		lodging
			nudging
all	fall		
	hall	er	jerk
	tall		herd
	ball		Bert
			hers
alt	halt		
	malt	ew	new
	Walt		stew
	altogether		brew
			slew
ar	art		
	ark	ge	rag – rage
	car		hug – huge
	farm		pigeon
			forge
aw	jaw		charge
	law		
	dawn	gi	raging
	hawk		waging
			ranging
ay	day		changing
	lay		
	say	ild	mild
	tray		wild
			child
ci	social		
	special	ind	find
	precious		kind
	vicious		mind
	gracious		bind
ci	cinder	ir	sir
	mincing		shirt
	icing		girl
	citizen		first

Figure 9-2   Word–pattern cards (part 5 of 7)

Vowel and Consonant Combinations (continued)

Front	Back	Front	Back
old	bold	some	someone
	cold		somehow
	fold		handsome
	mold		lonesome
oll	toll		something
	poll	squ	squirt
	scroll		squirm
	stroll		squint
olt	jolt		squiggle
	bolt	su	treasure
	colt		pleasure
	molt		measure
or	fork		usual
	born	ti	station
	torch		action
	storm		nation
ow	low		mention
	row		education
	slow	tu	nature
	throw		future
ow	cow		stature
	crown		picture
	growl		mixture
	down	ur	fur
oy	boy		spur
	Roy		church
	joy		hurl
	toy	wa	want
qu	ill	swa	water
	quill		wander
	quilt		swan
	quiet		swamp
	quite	wor	work
si	mansion		worse
	expression		worry
	occasion		worm
	pension		
	vision		

Figure 9-2 Word–pattern cards (part 6 of 7)

Silent Letters

Front	Back	Front	Back
Silent b	lamb	Silent k	knob
	doubt		knife
	limb		know
	numb		knelt
			knuckle
Silent g	gnat	Silent l	half
	gnaw		calf
	gnash		yolk
	gnome		calm
Silent gh	though	Silent t	jostle
	brought		rustle
	bought		gristle
	height		bustle
	straight		
Silent h	ghost	Silent w	wreath
	ghetto		wrestle
	rhyme		wrong
	rhubarb		wrinkle
	rhinoceros		

Figure 9-2   Word–pattern cards (part 7 of 7)

When you first show these cards to your child, have him read the front and back sides to you. As you go through the cards, make two piles. In one pile, put the word patterns that he knows very well. In the other pile, put the word patterns that he stumbles on. If he doesn't read the card correctly, say the word pattern and illustrative words slowly and clearly as you move your finger underneath the letters from left to right across the card:

Pronounce all the words on the cards distinctly the way they are spelled. Give the vowels true sounds—*a* as in *ant*, *e* as in *egg*, *i* as in *ink*, *o* as in *otter*, and *u* as in *up*.

Don't teach what dictionaries and educators refer to as the "schwa" sound, designated by an upside down e (ə). This symbol has been assigned to all the sloppy vowels in conversational speech. When we talk fast, we change the true letter sounds in the words. For example, we say *pensul* instead of *pencil*. But if you give the vowels regular sounds when you say the words, your child will learn to read and spell correctly. The so-called schwa will only confuse him. As a result, the only schwa sound you'll teach is for the little article, *a*, since this is its dictionary pronunciation.

Be very critical when you judge your child's understanding of the word patterns. He must have an automatic response to each one to indicate mastery. At the end of the first lesson, you'll know the combinations that he's never learned. If you find he's never learned the beginning sounds for the letters or the most common sight words, go back to chapter 8 and begin with these. Don't assume that he knows the basic skills. Check it out.

Begin the next lesson with the combinations that your child doesn't know. Always use the back of each card to make the letter-sound relationship clear. These words illustrate how these letter-sound patterns form words. They will train your child to automatically respond to each letter or letters with a sound.

Your child will also learn to note the differences in the beginning, middle, and end of each word and how they affect the pronunciation and meaning of the word. For example, he'll learn how the verb *confide* becomes the noun *confidence* when the *ence* ending is added to it. This skill enables him to see the smaller parts in long words. It lets him break words with many syllables down into recognizable parts. And that means he can figure out new words he encounters as he becomes a more advanced reader.

Jennifer constantly made mistakes as she read, such as reading *certain* for *caution*. She apparently had learned to recognize words by their shapes. Since both these words begin with c and have the same number of letters, they look somewhat the same (not to me, but they definitely did to her):

This told me that she didn't look at each letter as her eyes moved across the page.

I also discovered that she didn't know some of the most basic letter-and-sound combinations. Even if your child scores on the fourth-grade reading level or higher, be sure he knows these word patterns solidly. He must have this foundation to advance in reading.

On the first day of the reading program, it took twenty minutes to show Jennifer the word-pattern cards. We read for only ten minutes and stopped. Our half-hour lesson was over. The drill had tired both of us.

Each succeeding day, the amount of time spent on the cards grew less. At the end of the six weeks when she knew all the combinations thoroughly, we still went through all the cards, but we used only five to ten minutes of the reading lesson for them because now her responses were automatic.

Read, read, read

After you've gone through the flash cards, spend the rest of the half hour listening to your child read to you. It's when he reads that he applies his knowledge of the word patterns to decode words and get meaning from the printed page. As you listen to him read, you give him the individualized help he needs to correct the bad habits he's acquired. If he has no bad habits, you help him add to his present skill development.

Two questions confront you at this point. One is what to read, and the other is how to correct your child's problems with reading.

First, what to read

Your child needs to read books that frustrate him a little to cause him to use new skills. He needs to begin to decode more difficult words and to become familiar with more complicated sentence structures. When he reads on a more frustrating level, he's forced to discard his whole-word methods of decoding. Out of necessity, he must use word-pattern skills to separate the words into recognizable parts.

Primarily, the books that you use to teach him these skills should entertain, amuse, or inform him. If your child thinks reading is fun, he'll be motivated to try to apply the various decoding techniques that he has learned. So choose one of the classics or prize-winning children's books with a story written in language that forces him to use decoding skills as it provides the enjoyment of reading.

If you plan to use this reading program to teach your third-grade child more advanced skills, you can choose from many interesting books for your lessons. At this level, he hasn't been exposed to all the standard primary-grade books. At the library, select one that's color-coded higher than his present reading level to make him reach out to absorb new vocabulary. This way his reading will gradually reinforce the word patterns you teach him.

But if you plan to do remedial work with an older child on the third-grade level, these books will have lost their appeal. Either he'll say, "That's a baby book" or "I saw a filmstrip on that" or "My teacher read that to us." To motivate him, you must choose books that are new to him.

I tested this program on a neighbor's eleven-year-old child. Sarah was in the sixth grade but read poorly on the third-grade level. She enjoyed *Meet John F. Kennedy*, *Football Players Do Amazing Things*, and *Magicians Do Amazing Things* from the Step-Up Books by Random House. These books average 70 pages each and offer new information in large-print, readable text. The sentences are short, but the vocabulary is not too limited. After she had mastered letter-sound decoding skills, Sarah gained confidence and eliminated most of her bad habits with these books. She could read them quickly and get a feeling of success and satisfaction. If your child is in the primary grades or if he's older and needs to practice, he'll love the biographies and science books in this series.

Jennifer, who tested on the fourth-grade level, began with *Heidi*, the classic by Johanna Spyri. I like it so much that my enthusiasm carried her through it, but she had difficulty with the vocabulary and the sentence structure. This made it a good teaching device but not always a pleasant reading experience for her. However, she could identify with the feelings of the little girl when she had to leave her grandfather and when she began to learn to read. *Heidi* touched her as no other book that she had ever read. She needed to know that books have emotional appeal.

Other frustration-level books for ten- to twelve-year-olds might be *The Black Stallion* by William Farley or *Big Red* by Jim Kjelgaard. These animal stories have universal attraction. Sarah and Jennifer both enlarged their vocabularies pleasurably with these two classics.

Books that tell how to do something and those that have riddles and jokes also furnish special motivation to read. And history and math texts, as well as biographies and science books, interest many children at all ages. May Hill Arbuthnot's *Children's Reading in the Home* and Nancy Larrick's *A Parent's Guide to Reading* will provide you with additional titles to hold the attention of your child.

Since the books you choose for your reading lessons will be slightly advanced for your child, don't expect him to read with absolute understanding. However, check that he has a general idea of the characters, setting, and plot in each book. At the start of the reading program, Jennifer couldn't understand any dialects. The words simply did not make pictures for her. We read half of *Treasure Island* by Robert Louis Stevenson before I realized that she couldn't tell me what had happened in previous chapters. When the characters spoke in English slang, she didn't have any idea what they said. My explanations as she read didn't help to create a continuous flow of images. After this realization, we changed to a book with a more familiar setting that she could visualize easily after she decoded the words.

In short, remember that you want to make this learning experience as pleasant as you can. If the book is too difficult and frustrates too much or if it doesn't sustain your child's interest, choose another. But always be sure to choose one that's slightly advanced for your child so he'll get plenty of practice in using the word patterns to decode new words.

How to correct your child's problems with reading

If your child has no reading problem, this program will quickly raise his reading level as it clarifies his own conclusions about word patterns and adds to his present knowledge. When you read together during your scheduled lessons, you'll share the joy of books. He'll read more fluently as he gradually improves his skills. For both of you, it should be a time to strengthen your relationship as well as to practice reading.

But if your child is an older reader and has developed bad habits, expect to be annoyed and irritated when he reads to you. I have unlimited patience in the classroom, but with Jennifer, my irritation showed. She knew me well enough to interpret my body language to mean that her mistakes in reading frustrated me. Furthermore, she felt this meant I didn't like her.

In my work with Jennifer and Sarah, I experienced very different emotional reactions. Sarah displayed negative behavior in school but came to me with an eagerness to learn. She relaxed with me and gained skills and confidence daily. In contrast, Jennifer began each lesson with a hostile attitude and became visibly more nervous with each of my corrections.

I didn't like to make her unhappy. But I knew that to help her I had to break her bad habits. I had to tell her when she made a mistake even though for awhile she felt like a failure and got angry. Consequently, for the first six weeks, we could not read pleasantly for more than a half hour.

Most of the incorrect reading habits of your child will spontaneously disappear when he learns accurate decoding skills. But it will require diligent, consistent effort on your part. Prepare yourself for your role as teacher. Accept the fact that you may encounter hostility in your child. Remember that you'll have to help him overcome his patterns of failure. It won't be easy. But when he sees he can do it and reading becomes pleasurable, his negative feelings will go away with his bad habits.

After you've gone through the word cards, then, ask your child to read aloud the book that you've selected. Oral reading enables him to hear his own errors. As he reads, he notices that he has made mistakes. But often he doesn't know how to change his incorrect patterns. As you listen, you'll give him the individual help that will cause him to change.

If your child's a poor reader, he can't accurately decode words. However, he still tries to make sense of the symbols on the page. When he reads aloud, he mispronounces words because he doesn't know the letter-and-sound correspondences. He leaves words out altogether. He frequently adds little words, such as *the*, *to*, *at*, and *this*, to give him time to think and figure out the meaning. He misreads small, often-used words, such as *when* for *then* and *that* for *what*. He loses his place. The incoherent result frays your nerves as you listen to him read.

He feels that he must hurry. He's been told that he reads "too slowly." Since he didn't know how to read faster when he was first told this, he began to use techniques to make him sound fluent. These methods didn't work, but he didn't know what else to do. Now, he needs help to discard these bad habits.

First, slow him down. Tell him that he must look at each word carefully in order to figure it out. Ask him to put his finger on each word as he reads.

I could not get Jennifer or Sarah to "finger-point." They'd been ridiculed for this habit and regarded it as "baby behavior." For the first six weeks, they placed a 3 x 5 card under each line of type and moved it down as they read. This helped them to stay on the same line. When they lost their places, they didn't have to look all over the page. It was a real breakthrough, however, when they finally agreed to touch each word because then they took each one as a unit, decoded it accurately, and went on to the next one.

Each developed her own solution to the need to do this. Jennifer held her book up so that she could use the tip of a pencil to follow under each word and no one could see it. Sarah rested her open hand on the page and then moved all her fingers in a fan-pattern as she kept her eyes on one fingertip under each word.

When they no longer needed to concentrate so carefully on each word, they gave up these crutches. We must not decide when children are ready to discard a learning tool. When a child learns to ride a bike and you run alongside to steady him, he begs, "Don't let go—I'll fall." When he's ready, he says, "Now, let me try it alone." Reading is another learning experience that requires aids to succeed.

Each time before he begins to read, remind your child to stop when he sees a period and take a rest when he sees a comma. Tell him that it will help him to understand what he reads if he gets the meaning from one group of words at a time. When he pauses for punctuation, he also slows down his reading.

Next, at the first lesson, tell your child to read the little word *a* as *uh*. When I started this program with Jennifer, she pronounced it as long *a*. As a result, her oral reading had a stilted phrasing, and she misread many words that began with the letter *a*. It took eight lessons to change this response, and it seemed that I stopped her on it one thousand times. The day that she consistently read *a* as *uh*, we hugged each other, and I treated her to an ice cream cone on the spot.

You must change this habit in your child right away because long *a* is not the most common sound for the letter *a*. At the beginning of many often-used sight words, it is *uh*, as in *away*, *about*, *again*, *around*, etc. In the middle and the end of long words, it is frequently *uh*. Examples are per-ma-nence, pro-pa-gan-da, and for-mu-la.

Finger-pointing will cause your child to concentrate on one word at a time. Observing punctuation marks will help him slow down and absorb several words at a time. Reading the word *a* as *uh* will improve his phrasing and sounding-out of words with the letter *a* in them. Begin immediately to make your child aware of these important reading skills.

Finally, and most important, do not permit your child to read inaccurately. Jennifer and Sarah consistently misread words because they didn't look closely at each letter. For example, they said *his* for *this*, *bind* for *blind*, and *house* for *horse*. Always, I called their attention to the letters on the page. Basically, they knew the letters and sounds, but they tended to read whole words and not see the significant letter differences in each one. As your child reads, simply point out the letter-and-sound correspondence of the words every time he makes a mistake.

It's true that when you teach your child the word patterns, you give him proper skills. But he can't immediately stop using the techniques that have gotten him through school until now. You must gradually show him how to use these words patterns to read.

So refer to the word patterns of the cards as you read with your child. For example, if your child can't decode *fraudulent*, remind him that the letters *au* say *au* as in *haul*. Then, show him the syllables. Write the word on an index card as *fraud-u-lent*. Help him to separate long words into known parts.

Call his attention to the plural endings and verb changes. Every letter has significance. Don't let him glide past these important differences.

Praise him when he accurately decodes a new word even if the spoken pronunciation is not the same. Encourage him to read the words as they are spelled. Later, he'll remember how to spell words like *hand-ker-chief* if he reads it differently than he says it.

You see, at this point, we're trying to get the child to look carefully at the letters he reads. Once he becomes a fluent reader, he'll pronounce the words correctly when he reads aloud. But as a beginner or as a child with reading problems, he needs to pay special attention to the letters and give them regular sounds. If he does, he'll be able to figure out any word that he encounters in his reading, no matter how many syllables it has.

Don't let him rely on context clues. Educators tell us that as we read, we anticipate the next word according to the sense of the sentence. Your child has been taught this technique to enable him to guess at words. For example, when he reads a book about a farm, and the sentence is "The horse stood in the b _____ ," he expects that the next word will be *barn*. However, it could be *barnyard*, *brook*, *bucket*, or any other word beginning with *b*. Always point out the letter-and-sound patterns in the words to show him that reading is logical.

Don't let him skip words, don't let him add words, and don't let him substitute words. Tell him over and over that the letters give all the necessary clues to read accurately. Tell him to "read only the words on the page."

All the bad habits will disappear as your child learns reading skills. If he looks at each word and decodes it accurately, he'll stop omitting, adding, and substituting words. As he moves from word to word across the page, he'll no longer reverse letters or lose his place or repeat the same words. As he practices and refines his skills, he'll begin to get meaning from the print.

Very soon, then, you'll notice changes in your child's ability to read. No one will have to tell you he's improved. You'll see little signs that tell you that letters have new meaning to him.

Jennifer surprised me when she started to read the newspaper as it lay out on the breakfast table. It had been there all her life, but the words had never leaped out at her and captured her interest before.

Now, too, she began to read the cereal boxes, the labels on the shampoo and lotion bottles, and the directions to the Monopoly game. Each day she became more involved with words.

Sarah's improvement was evident day-by-day in her school-work. She'd taken a remediation course in summer school and was in a remedial reading group during the year. But after eight half-hour sessions with me, she scored 100 percent on a pre-test to divide words into syllables. On the ninth day, she came and told me that now she was able to finish her language arts papers in the allotted time.

At each lesson, she had more triumphs to report. The following week, she said, "Now I can remember what I read." And then she found that she could spell because "now I can sound out words."

Don't expect all of your child's reading problems to disappear overnight, though. Sarah, for example, continued to have trouble reading aloud; her oral reading lacked smoothness. It's true that she made a lot of progress in the first six weeks we worked together. When she was able to read each word accurately, she began to read in groups of words. And as her eyes took in three or more words at a time, her phrasing improved. But she still felt she had to rush. I constantly reminded her to "slow down." So even though her reading ability improved dramatically, it took much more than six weeks for her to feel comfortable when she read aloud. All those years of failure could not be erased in such a short time.

After six weeks

Thus, in spite of the progress they'd made, I could see that Jennifer and Sarah both needed to do more reading to increase their vocabularies and to become more fluent in their word-recognition skills. So after six weeks, I continued the lessons with each of them, but I varied the format.

When they could read all of the word-pattern cards in less than 15 minutes and their worst habits in reading had disappeared, I began to dictate words to them. Each day, instead of beginning with the word-pattern cards, I started the lesson with a spelling exercise.

Reading and writing are reversible skills, but writing requires more effort. When your child reads, he need only look at the letters and associate the appropriate sounds with them to recognize the words. When he writes, he must think of the sounds of the words, associate the letters that say them, and remember the shape of the letters to reproduce them on paper. If he knows how to write, he will be able to read better.

That's why, now that Sarah and Jennifer knew the word-pattern cards, we began to use their knowledge to practice spelling. They numbered their papers from 1 to 20. Then I dictated words that illustrated the letter-and-sound correspondences they had learned.

Figure 9-3 is the first exercise I used. Numbers 1, 2, and 3 are words with the ur pattern—curl, Thursday, and Saturday. (I wanted them to know how to spell the basics—the days of the week, the months of the year, the states, the continents, the oceans, etc.—and I kept that in mind when I made up the spelling lists.)

Numbers 4, 5, and 6 vary the ea sound—beak, break, and beast. Numbers 7 and 8 illustrate the or combination—snort and short. Then, 9, 10, and 11 ask for the ou sound in mound, flour, and mouth. (Interestingly enough, Jennifer and Sarah wrote both flour and flower, showing me they knew they could spell the ending sound with either our or ower. I didn't give them sample sentences because my goal was to teach them that they could spell by sounding out words.)

The last nine words in the list have the same vowel sound, but it's spelled in different ways. Numbers 12, 13, and 14 require the understanding of aw in jaw, shawl, and crawl. Then, 15 and 16 are all and stall. And the list ends with the au word pattern in haul, Paul, August, and Australia.

Each day I gave them a similar list of words to spell that drew on their understanding and application of the letter-and-sound combinations.

I found that Jennifer and Sarah couldn't always tell when to use the long vowel sound and when to use the short vowel sound. So I included din-dinner and dine-diner in one exercise. Notice that

1. curl		11. mouth
2. Thursday		12. jaw
3. Saturday		13. shawl
4. beak		14. crawl
5. break		15. all
6. beast		16. stall
7. snort		17. haul
8. short		18. Paul
9. mound		19. August
10. flour		20. Australia

Figure 9-3   Spelling exercise #1

dinner has two n's and *diner*, only one. *Sup, supper,* and *super* also illustrate that the vowel sounds change when the consonant in the middle of the word is double or single.

I varied the beginnings and endings of words in the lists to train their ears to hear the differences and their minds to write the corresponding letters. For example, I used *picture* and *mixture* for differences in beginning and middle sounds and sameness in endings; and *sure* and *sugar* for similarity in beginning sounds and differences in endings. Always I spoke slowly and distinctly, giving each combination a true sound.

You can use figures 9-3 through 9-12 as spelling exercises for your child. The words in these lists have been selected to show your child how words are formed. They'll build his confidence in his ability to sound out words. They'll end his confusion in spelling. And they'll tell you how well he understands the letter-and-sound association.

In place of the drill with the word-pattern cards, dictate these spelling exercises at the beginning of each lesson. Have your child number his paper from 1 to 20. Then, read the words aloud to him. Pronounce each word first as we say it in conversation. Then, pronounce each word again with true vowels as we read and spell it.

It will take ten minutes to administer these exercises. After your child has mastered them, you can dictate your own sentences or even a few lines from a book or magazine.

1. mad	11. bake
2. made	12. mistake
3. boat	13. social
4. float	14. special
5. piece	15. wrap
Rule: Put "i" before "e" except after "c" or in words that sound like "neighbor" and "weigh."	16. wrench
	17. blue
	18. Tuesday
6. pier	19. city
7. pledge	20. cities
8. judge	Rule: Change "y" to "i" and add "es" (or "er" or "ed").
9. bread	
10. breakfast	

Figure 9-4 Spelling exercise #2

1. man	11. settlement
2. mane	12. knee
3. manner	13. general
4. sent	14. generate
5. sentence	15. fact
6. rat	16. face
7. rate	17. factory
8. separate	18. exit
9. set	19. exist
10. settle	20. expect

Figure 9-5 Spelling exercise #3

1. teach
2. teacher
3. underneath
4. failure
5. berry
6. blueberries

   Rule: Change "y" to "i" and add "es."

7. change
8. exchange
9. exchanging

   Rule: Drop the final "e" and add "ing."

10. vanilla
11. Washington
12. Valentine
13. Thanksgiving
14. mud
15. muddle
16. ban
17. banner
18. August
19. Austria
20. Africa

Figure 9-6 Spelling exercise #4

1. oil
2. choice
3. fool
4. choose
5. feel
6. screen
7. meal
8. scream
9. peach
10. preach
11. watch
12. water
13. ear
14. clear
15. eight

   Rule: Put "i" before "e" except after "c" or in words that sound like "neighbor" and "weigh."

16. neighbor
17. thrill
18. quill
19. sink
20. blink

Figure 9-7 Spelling exercise #5

1. joy	11. lug
2. joyous	12. luggage
3. owl	13. day
4. scowl	14. crayon
5. queer	15. every
6. steer	16. everyone
7. out	17. suit
8. scout	18. suitable
9. find	19. chair
10. blindfold	20. dairy

Figure 9-8   Spelling exercise #6

1. burn	12. din
2. murder	13. dinner
3. first	14. dine
4. birthday	15. diner
5. Atlanta	16. come
6. Atlantic	17. coming
7. Antarctica	Rule: Drop the final "e" and add "ing."
8. America	
9. car	18. commit
10. carton	19. committee
11. person	20. competition

Figure 9-9   Spelling exercise #7

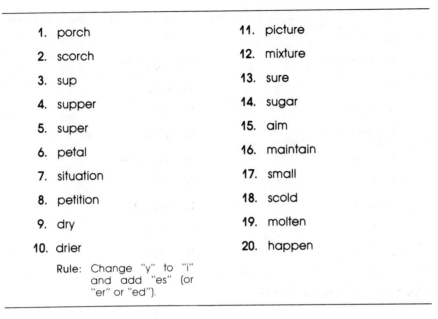

1. porch
2. scorch
3. sup
4. supper
5. super
6. petal
7. situation
8. petition
9. dry
10. drier
    Rule: Change "y" to "i" and add "es" (or "er" or "ed").

11. picture
12. mixture
13. sure
14. sugar
15. aim
16. maintain
17. small
18. scold
19. molten
20. happen

Figure 9-10 Spelling exercise #8

1. United
2. Pacific
3. Indian
4. January
5. plunge
6. plunging
    Rule: Drop the final "e" and add "ing."

7. dance
8. trace
9. field
    Rule: Put "i" before "e" except after "c" or in words that sound like "neighbor" and "weigh."

10. receive
11. crow
12. know
13. worth
14. calm
15. dungeon
16. strange
17. famous
18. delicious
19. though
20. thought

Figure 9-11 Spelling exercise #9

1.	February	11.	plate
2.	Wednesday	12.	platter
3.	night	13.	want
4.	bright	14.	wander
5.	phone	15.	gloomy
6.	photograph	16.	fancy
7.	reply	17.	action
8.	cycle	18.	nation
9.	thumb	19.	active
10.	doubt	20.	massive

Figure 9-12 Spelling exercise #10

After the spelling exercise, continue to use the rest of the half hour in reading with your child. By now, his oral reading should be smooth and confident. Once he looks closely at each word, he recognizes when he has made errors because he fails to get meaning. He then corrects himself. He'll go back to the beginning of a sentence if necessary to read it accurately.

As I mentioned before, though, some children take longer to get to this point than others. Jennifer and Sarah both took eight weeks to reach this level of fluency. During our lessons, I continued to follow along as they read until they could see their own mistakes and voluntarily corrected themselves. Then I let them read to me without my direct supervision. Sarah said that this practice in reading aloud gave her confidence for the times when she had to read to her classmates in school.

Sometimes, she and Jennifer read alternating pages to me from a library book. This way they improved their expressive phrasing and learned from each other's reading.

Now that they had decoding skills, the girls could correctly sound out any word. But they couldn't always explain what it meant. So as we read together, we concentrated more on vocabulary and meaning.

As children read, they develop an understanding for the words they encounter frequently. This explains why they can sometimes define a word in the context of a sentence but not on a vocabulary test. However, as they advance in school, such context clues don't always work. Unfamiliar words such as *repast* and *immerse* must be looked up in a dictionary.

I like *Webster's Intermediate Dictionary* (G. & C. Merriam Co., 1977) because it was prepared especially for students in the middle grades. Its broad range of vocabulary includes words in today's news, current events, and textbooks. Each word is divided into syllables as it's listed alphabetically. (Not all dictionaries do this today. This separation helps your child find words more quickly as it makes each word more readable.) Next, it gives a general American pronunciation with a simple, diacritical key on each righthand page. The part-of-speech label follows just as in an adult dictionary. Most important, the definitions are clear and readable with sentences that illustrate the meanings. Furthermore, children can hold and use it comfortably because it's 7 inches wide and 9-1/2 inches long.

When we began our lessons, I looked up the words in the dictionary for Jennifer and Sarah as we read to be sure that I defined the words they didn't understand accurately for them. Since there were so many words they didn't know, I did this to avoid spending our reading time with dictionary skills.

As they read regularly, the same words continued to appear. Soon they learned the meanings of these words and consequently reduced the number of unfamiliar words. When they reached this level of comprehension, they began to look up their own words.

In short, as Jennifer and Sarah read more, their vocabularies increased. They were able to understand their social studies texts for the first time and to retain information that they read. Both reported that they could spell better. I could see they could write better. Together we recounted their daily triumphs in class—the now-correct language arts exercises, the now-easily-done writing papers, the now-quickly-completed reading assignments.

Unfortunately, the school didn't notice right away that they had improved. But slowly, their steady progress was rewarded. In spring, their standardized achievement scores were up two levels for Sarah and one level for Jennifer. And when report cards came out, both had improved in all their subjects but especially in reading.

The point is, don't get discouraged if no one else notices your child's improvement as quickly as you do. Be patient. And bolster your child's confidence by showing him that he's doing better all the time.

Continue to read together

Even with all their progress, the girls and I continued to read together. When Jennifer began to read to herself for periods of time without my prompting, I became more flexible about the lessons. (For quite a while, she read aloud to herself.) Now, we can sit in the same room and read together, only I have my book and she has hers. I need to be sure that she's reading often because I know that if she reads regularly, she'll extend her skills.

Of course, your child does read in school every day. And when he reads, he practices the new skills in reading that he's learned. If you question him, though, you'll find that he doesn't read very much in school.

So when he begins to read on his own, be sure that he spends a half hour four times a week in reading. He needs to practice his skills at least two hours a week to maintain his reading level and improve his vocabulary. Check on his fluency and have him read aloud from his current book while you prepare dinner or before he goes to bed. When he reads to you, you can help him with words that he doesn't understand. You can praise him for the good work that he now does. And you can be sure that he'll improve in school. You'll both benefit from this time with the written language.

Chapter **10**

How your child learns school behaviors that guarantee success

At the end of my daughter's fourth-grade year in school, her teacher told me that Jennifer "doesn't tune in" or "pay attention in class." "She doesn't finish her work." "She doesn't follow directions."

At other conferences when I taught school, I heard teachers tell parents that their children didn't have good self-concepts, that they didn't sit still, and that they couldn't work alone.

As a parent, I've bristled at these comments while wondering how to change my child. I've never heard a teacher tell a parent what to do about these unpleasant school behaviors. It seems that once your child has developed these characteristics, he displays them throughout his school years. Later, he becomes an under-achiever who doesn't work up to his potential.

As a teacher, I know these behaviors begin in the home. After each conference, I could see the roots for these classroom problems in the relationship between the parent and the child. In fact, many times the parent complained of the same problems with the child at home.

In contrast, some parents seem to know instinctively how to encourage behaviors that will lead to success in school.

Maricela was a bilingual girl in my first-grade class whose first language was Spanish. Her mother spoke little English, and her father had a heavy accent. Yet Maricela knew how to act in school. She listened attentively and finished her own work. In this

175

way, she learned the skills she needed to achieve beyond grade level. As a result, she had good feelings about herself.

When her parents came for the conference, they had Maricela sit with them to listen to the teacher's comments. In this way, they showed her that they considered her to be responsible for her own work. They smiled at her when they heard she was a good student. This is how they communicated to her that they considered school to be very important and that they approved of her efforts.

Her father confided to me that he read to Maricela every day, even though he worked long hours. He said he talked to her a lot and told her that she'd have to listen and try hard in order to succeed. He asked if there was anything they could do at home to assist the teacher.

While we talked, the baby sister played with some colorful, plastic blocks. When the conference ended, Maricela's mother told the sister in Spanish to "put the toys away." The family waited patiently while Maricela helped her slowly replace the blocks in a wicker basket and then return the basket to the shelf. When they finished, the parents smiled and praised them and then said goodbye.

I knew that Maricela would always do well in school because her family gave her clear messages about what they expected her to do. In fact, I was confident her little sister would follow in Maricela's footsteps; already her parents were showing her that they expected her to finish a task.

Maricela was such a contrast to Matt, the youngest of five children, whose parents were prosperous and educated. Testing by the school psychologist had shown that Matt had a large vocabulary, although he spoke little. A physical by his family doctor had indicated normal hearing. Other tests found that he had above-average capabilities. Yet he didn't pay attention in class, didn't finish his work, and hadn't learned to read at all.

When he arrived with his mother for the parent conference, he had two little cars in his pockets. He promptly sat down and began to make noises like a motor as he raced them on the floor. He seemed to be in his own world. His mother told him to move away from us so we could talk.

As I related how Matt didn't listen or follow directions, she nodded her head in agreement. Then, she told me he acted the same way at home so that now she never asked him to do anything. She said that he mainly watched television and played with his cars when he came home from school.

She asked me if he needed special help—if there was someplace she could take him to change his behavior. When I suggested that she read to him and help him learn his letters and sounds, she told me she didn't have time.

When we had finished talking, she urged Matt to button his coat and tie his shoelaces. But she didn't stop and wait for him to do these things, and he dragged out in his usual disarray.

Just as I knew that Maricela would be a good student, I could predict that Matt would have difficulty all through school. Already, he didn't function on grade level. He had "tuned out" and given up.

Yet each child *can* have the appropriate school behaviors that will insure success in school. If we only look at what's significant, we can prepare our children to learn at their optimum level.

How your child learns to listen

Before your child began to speak, he listened to others talk. He babbled to reproduce the sounds that he heard. When he murmured, "ma-ma-ma," you smiled and said, "Mama, that's right, Mama."

By doing this, you told him that you liked what he did. You encouraged him to make that sound again. You indicated to him that this combination of sounds had special meaning. You showed him that you wanted him to communicate with his world. He, in turn, listened to you and modified his babbling to produce intelligible speech.

Listening precedes speaking. It's a learned skill. It develops in the home through the interaction of the family members. When one person talks and the other listens, the child learns that communication is a two-way process.

If you say real things to your child, he learns to pay close attention to what you say. If you listen to him, you show him that his ideas are valuable. In contrast, if you don't listen to him and if you don't say anything that requires him to listen, he loses interest in the process. If you don't encourage his natural desire to communicate, he starts to "tune out."

The children in my kindergarten language group (described in chapter 5) did not listen for two reasons. First, they'd been ignored in their homes. No one ever spoke to them and expected an answer. They'd never been rewarded in any way for listening. Second, they had very small vocabularies. Most of the time, they didn't have a clear understanding of what they heard.

When these children talked to me, I listened carefully and responded to them. They learned to pay attention to me because I said meaningful things to them. Furthermore, they knew that I would smile and praise them if they listened. They had never received positive feedback for listening before.

As the days passed, what they heard rewarded them for listening. As their vocabularies grew, they were able to pay close attention when I spoke to them. They could now follow my directions because the words had meaning for them. They could listen to me read for a longer period of time because they could understand the stories better.

As your child's first teacher, you can easily and naturally teach him to be a good listener. When you ask him questions and listen to his answers, you encourage him to pay attention to what you say. When you give him information that interests him, he learns to listen carefully to absorb it. When you exchange ideas about his world with him, you teach him the value of communication, of listening as well as talking.

When you ask him to do an errand for you, you teach him how to follow directions. He must focus on what he hears to accomplish the task. You begin when he's very young with one-step requests. "Please get my purse from the kitchen table." Later, you tell him to "get my purse from the kitchen table, take 20 cents for milk for your lunch, and then bring my wallet to me." As your child understands more language and is able to carry out your commands, you give him longer directives. He must listen carefully to do them right.

If you teach your child to memorize nursery rhymes, you show him again how to listen carefully. He must pay attention to the words to remember them. He also learns new vocabulary that causes him to better understand what other people say.

If you play records for him, you encourage him to notice the differences in the sounds that he hears. He learns to recognize voices and musical instruments as he learns to reproduce some of these sounds.

If you read to your child, you give him the ultimate listening experience. Books enlarge his vocabulary and his knowledge of the world. They introduce him to emotions and situations that he'd never understand otherwise.

When you talk to your child and listen to him, you tell him about the communication process. When you teach him words through books and records, you prepare him to pay attention in school. You stimulate his curiosity to learn more ... and to learn more, he has to listen.

How your child learns to be independent

Very early in your child's life, he indicates to you when he's ready to do something for himself. For example, he grabs the spoon from your hand to feed himself. He takes his clothes off so he can learn to put them on. He climbs out of the stroller so he can push it himself. When he starts to talk, he says, "Me do it," and protests mightily when you refuse to let him.

Encourage your child to be independent when he shows that he's ready. Permit him to learn to do things by himself. Give him skills so that he can accomplish tasks.

When Timothy's mother brought him to my kindergarten class, she helped him take off his coat and boots. She didn't expect him to be able to do things for himself. She told me that he couldn't dress himself or feed himself. As a result, Timothy didn't even try but waited for his mother to help him. After she left school each morning, he refused to participate in group activities. He couldn't function without his mother. At the end of the year, he was retained in kindergarten because he couldn't do the tasks that his same-age classmates performed easily.

We teach our children to be independent and responsible when we let them do things for themselves. Slowly, they learn to eat and dress without assistance, to take a bath and use the toilet alone, and to utilize their free time in productive ways. Gradually, they add to the skills that enable them to take care of themselves.

When we don't let them acquire these skills, we deprive them of the independence they need for success. In school, each child must think, speak, read, and write by himself. If he begins at an early age to assume his personal responsibilities, he'll be able to master the academic skills later.

How your child learns to complete a task

When your child helps you put canned goods on the shelves in the kitchen cupboards, he sees you discharge a duty to the family. He observes completion of a task. Later, when you help him put his toys away in their places, he learns to take on his own duties in the household. He gets into the habit of finishing a job.

Like all skills, learning how to finish a job is something a child accomplishes in gradual and sequential steps, successfully completing one level before moving to another. Unfortunately, as parents, we don't always keep this in mind.

Sometimes, we expect too much from our children. We ask them to complete tasks when they haven't acquired enough skills. For example, we may give our child a puzzle that has too many parts or with pieces that are too small for him to grasp and turn easily. Perhaps it's so complicated that he can't remember what the puzzle should look like when it's finished. When you see that your child doesn't complete a task, determine whether it's too difficult for him.

Sometimes, we don't allow enough time for our child to finish. He never gets the feeling of satisfaction that comes with completion. He may be halfway through a project when we say, "Hurry up, it's time to go to the store." Try to tell him in advance that you must leave. Give him a chance to achieve his goal.

Sometimes, we overwhelm our child by the size of the assignment we give him. For example, if we ask a preschool (and even older) child to clean his room all by himself, we require more than he can do.

However, if we break the job into manageable parts, he may be able to accomplish it. For example, first, direct him to put all the blocks away and praise him for that accomplishment. Then, ask him to return the books to the bookshelf and praise him when he's done it. Finally, tell him to sort all the puzzles into their containers and praise him for that job. Each time he does a part of the clean-up well, he receives a reward for his efforts that makes him feel he can do the next part of the assignment.

This way you also teach your child how to divide a task into steps that can be carried out one at a time. If you've allowed enough time and wait until he finishes, he can experience the pleasures that come with completion. If your expectations are reasonable, he'll be assured of success.

Then, when he starts school, he'll have the confidence that he can follow directions and finish a job successfully. He won't be discouraged when his teacher asks him to do something he's never tried before. You will have given him skills that help him succeed.

How your child learns to have quiet moments

Eric had undergone tests for hyperactivity before he came to my kindergarten class. He had a short attention span, didn't listen, couldn't focus or finish a task, constantly came to me for reassurance, couldn't sit still or be quiet. But the tests indicated that he wasn't hyperactive.

After six months in my class, the school nurse observed him. She marveled at the change in his behavior. Now he worked alone to complete a puzzle or build with blocks. He sat quietly and listened for a reasonable length of time. He raised his hand when he wanted attention. He was calm and relaxed.

"How do you explain it?" she asked me. I reminded her of his family history. His parents were divorced, and he shifted from one parent to the other and to the grandmother. In one year, he had moved four times in the same neighborhood. His mother worked and had a busy business and social schedule. The school nurse agreed that his behavior had reflected the confusion in his home.

In the classroom, I had followed several guidelines that you can use to modify the active behavior of your child.

Have a regular routine. Children relax when they know what to expect. You don't have to live every day in a rigid pattern, but if your household has a predictable rhythm, your child will be more at ease. If you give him clear messages on what you want him to do and how you want him to act, he'll be better able to conform to your standards.

Simplify the learning environment. We can't protect our child from family hardships. They're part of life. But we can structure some elements of his daily existence to reduce the bewilderment he feels.

For example, remove toys that cause excessive, nervous movement. Noisy, battery-operated, mechanical toys cause confusion. They increase the chaos in the home. Eric was surrounded with gadgets and push-button toys. He brought a new gun or car to school often. But his mother wouldn't let him have crayons because she said he didn't know what to do with them.

Reduce the amount of television that your child watches. Studies have documented that children imitate the aggressive behavior they see in cartoons, mysteries, and westerns. Observe your child closely after he looks at television for two hours. See if he displays more active behavior. Karate kicks, angry talk, and pushing and shoving usually occur immediately after a child has seen aggressive behavior on television ... no matter whether he's seen a brief episode or watched for a long period of time. Furthermore, he'll remember what he's seen and imitate this aggressive behavior for a long time afterwards.

Show your child how to enjoy quiet activities. Sit with him and let him experiment with markers and crayons. Show him how to use them only on paper. Each time you give him this opportunity, he'll learn the appropriate ways to enjoy them.

Select the best quiet activity of all and read to your child. As I've said again and again throughout this book, reading teaches him in many ways all at the same time. When you read to him daily, he extends his attention span. He concentrates more as he absorbs language skills. He learns to appreciate the pleasures of a quiet time as you and he examine a book together.

Some children are more active than others. But we frequently reinforce this activity when we accept the notion that this is his personality and this is all he likes to do. You can teach your child to enjoy quiet pursuits. You'll find his excessive activity will be reduced when he learns to substitute other pastimes for those of aimlessness.

How your child develops a good self-concept

Allison was a sullen, unhappy girl in my first-grade class who didn't pay attention, didn't finish her work, and didn't achieve on grade level. As her mother and I talked at the parent conference, Allison made a little drawing. She brought it to me, and I praised her and said, "Oh, I like the colors you used. It's so cheerful." Her mother said, "Look at the way you wrote your name. The letters are all crowded together."

Your child decides if he has ability from the messages he receives from his world. If he does something and it turns out right, he concludes that he's capable. If it doesn't turn out right, he decides he's not capable and should give up trying.

When he draws, he's unsure of what a drawing should look like. He can't put on the paper what he sees in his head. But he wants to communicate. He wants to get better. He brings his drawing to us to get feedback about the value of his effort. If we praise and accept his attempt, we tell him that it has worth. We give him the message that he can succeed.

But many times we think that to teach him, we must criticize and offer suggestions. We feel that we must say something to improve the child's work. We find it hard to accept his best effort and approve of it.

Allison's mother had good intentions. She wanted Allison to learn how to write her name correctly. But that wasn't the message she gave Allison. She didn't tell Allison that she liked her drawing, and Allison concluded that her work didn't meet her mother's approval. Allison only heard that she hadn't printed her name well enough to please her mother.

Frank was also in my first-grade class. He worked slowly and laboriously as he tried to print. When he brought his paper to me at the end of the time period, I wrote "Excellent" at the top even though it wasn't finished. Each day he wrote more. Each day I smiled and wrote "Excellent" on his paper. When the first parent conference was held eight weeks later, Frank could print very well and completed all his writing assignments on time.

His mother said, "I couldn't understand how you could write 'Excellent' on his papers when he'd done only part of the assignment and formed his letters so poorly. But now his work is great. How did you do it?" I explained to her that at the beginning of the year Frank was doing his best work. I knew he'd continue to do his best and get better if I showed him that I liked what he did.

Praise and acceptance motivate children to do more. Your child wants to please you. Smile and tell him that you like what he does. When he feels he's succeeding, he'll want to do that same activity again. He'll want to get the good feelings that come when a job is done well. So he'll repeat the same thing until he masters it. Then, he'll have the confidence to try to do other things, so he'll go on to the next level of difficulty.

By the time your child comes to school, he's decided whether or not he can learn new things. He's already concluded whether he should try to compete with others to master new skills.

Help your child to have success. Tell him when you like what he does. Try to find the good things to call to his attention. When you tell him about these things, you give him a clear message about what's important to you. You indicate that he pleases you. And you encourage him to make the effort to succeed.

What you can do today

What can Matt's mother do for him now that he's in the first grade and has "tuned out?" First, she must accept the responsibility for some of his problems. If she accepts that he's learned to shut things out at home, she can examine her home learning environment and change it to teach him new behaviors.

She can begin to turn off the television and show him some alternate activities that will provide him with school-related skills, build his confidence, and create an interest in school. For example, she can give him small jobs at home that require him to listen and follow directions. She can give him enough time and wait for him to finish. Then she can show him that she likes what he's done.

She can change his free time to include books and paper-and-pencil tasks. When she shows him that she wants him to learn to read and write, he'll see that he can please her if he masters these skills. He'll want to practice with these materials to get better.

If she rewards him for his accomplishments with smiles and pleasant comments, he'll want to learn more. He'll conclude that it's fun to try new things. He'll see that he can understand his world—that there's no limit to what the world holds for him to explore.

When he can function in school, he'll get positive feedback that he's capable. He'll know that he has value—that he can compete with others. He'll respond to his environment with interest and enthusiasm. He'll begin the cycle of success.

You can help your child the same way. If he has problems in school, find out whether he has all the important school behaviors. Decide to help him become more independent and responsible for himself. Determine to show him that he can have success.

Chapter **11**

How you can keep your child learning

I started to read before I entered school. I don't remember when I learned. One day I just knew how to do it. To me, it was easy and fun.

When I went to school, though, no one knew I could read. In my reading group, I learned about the mechanics of reading, but I wondered why we did this. The books we had to use didn't tell a story, and I endured the time I spent in the group as we waited for our turn to read.

Yet I remember how much I enjoyed listening to my mother when she read *Peter Rabbit* and *Cinderella* and *The Three Bears* to me before I started school. I thrilled to the fright of Peter Rabbit when Mr. MacGregor chased him; I felt sad when he had to go to bed early and his good brothers and sisters had a treat. I looked forward to the story of Cinderella and how good triumphs over evil. I loved the sweet and gentle bears who found Goldilocks in their house. I was anxious to learn to read these books to myself.

When I was older, I recall my pleasure when a neighbor let me take some of her grown children's books home to read. It was summer, and I got lost in Hans Christian Andersen's *Fairy Tales*, *Alice in Wonderland*, and *Hans Brinker, Or, The Silver Skates*.

Later, I have the classroom memory of my teacher reading to us *The Call of the Wild* by Jack London and *A Christmas Carol* by Charles Dickens. The words took me to other places and times and created pictures that reached into my own experiences and increased their depth.

Finally, I remember that as I grew up, I read anything and everything. In a collection of plays, poems, and stories, I would first read the most appealing stories, but eventually I would read the entire book. In school after I finished my assignments, I would read history or geography texts if there were no other books in the room. I found that reading took me to a world of real and imagined pleasure. It was my reward and escape from the routine and details of life.

In my first-grade class, I had a quiet little boy named Lance whose experience seemed to parallel my own. He wanted to learn to read when he came to school and sat very still when I read to the class. Sometimes, he would tug on my sleeve afterwards and ask questions like, "What was the name of the boy in the story?" Or he would confide to me, "I have a park like that near my house."

However, he squirmed and daydreamed when he was in his reading group. He didn't like the drill we did on letters and sounds and plurals and verb endings. And while he did all the exercises in his workbook right, he took a long time to complete them. But as soon as he finished, he would go to my bookshelf and immediately become absorbed in a story. At the end of each school day, he signed out one of my books and read it to himself on the bus and to his mother or his older sister when he got home.

When he took his achievement test in spring, he had gained the highest reading score in my group—2.7 (second grade, seventh month). More important, he had established the reading habit and had developed a love of reading.

Both Lance and I wanted to learn how to read before we came to school. Someone in his home had awakened in him, as my mother had in me, an interest to find out what the printed words said. This interest grew as he continued to satisfy his curiosity about the world with books. And his skills grew—not so much in his reading group but in his outside reading.

Your child, too, will become a better reader by reading. His vocabulary will continue to expand as he encounters new words in his books. But how can you keep him growing and learning in the dynamic process of reading? How can you keep him reading?

Be sure he knows that reading is fun

When your child is very young and you read to him, you show him that books are a source of pleasure. Through books, he can get information and be entertained and amused. He finds that he clarifies his own experiences as he learns more about his world. As he continues to receive messages that he can get many different satisfactions from reading, he wants to learn to read by himself. He thinks of reading as a way to spend his free time.

If your child's only experiences with reading occur in school, he may conclude that it's drudgery. Unless he knows the many joys of reading, he won't want to try to become a better reader.

Start now to show your child that reading is fun. Even if he's older and knows how to read, he'll like it if you read to him.

Jennifer is eleven years old and still loves it when I read *Winnie-the-Pooh* or *The Little Prince* to her. Sometimes we take turns reading a book together. I read a page; then she reads the next. This way she gets to practice and also becomes a better listener. As I read with expression and meaningful phrasing, she learns the correct pronunciation of new vocabulary and hears the beauties and imageries of the language. When we talk about the story, she thinks more deeply about the author's meaning. And, of course, she reacts to my enthusiastic feelings about the book. Together we share a positive, relaxing experience.

Always read something you enjoy so that you're enthusiastic about the selection. If you read aloud with zest, you transmit your positive feelings about the book. You make it come alive. You show your child that this interaction with words is like a conversation between two people.

Select a wide variety of books that are personal and satisfying—that intrigue your child with words. Pick out stories that offer substance—that are about real people and real emotions so he can identify with the characters and experiences in the books he reads. Then, to arouse his imagination and higher ideals, choose some myths, legends, hero stories, and fairy tales. Present him with books that absorb him—whatever his personality. If you do, you'll find that sometimes when you must stop to do something else, your child will read on without you because he's become involved with the content.

Read to him from your newspaper or magazine. Share your own pleasant encounters with reading. In this way, you communicate to him that you use reading to enhance your everyday life. Many times, you'll stimulate him to read the item by himself.

Surround him with reading material

Have lots of magazines, newspapers, books, and paperbacks in your home. I specify paperbacks because they seem less like books to children who've had bad experiences with reading. In paperback form, you can find classics like *Pinocchio* and *Alice in Wonderland* as well as *Snoopy* and *Mad Libs*. And for children just starting to read, paperbacks offer a chance to buy inexpensively many of the favorites that they like to read over and over. At any rate, you'll encourage your child to read daily when you provide an abundance of materials that interest him.

There are many ways to supply your child with reading material. One of the best ways to get him to enjoy reading is to take him to the library. Let him browse and find books that answer his questions, that tell him how to do or make something, that amuse or inspire him, that take him to another time and place, that show him that his views about life are not isolated.

At the same time, help him select a book that he can read easily—one that matches his present skill development. If he experiences too much frustration, he won't enjoy reading.

If your child has already decided that he doesn't like to read, go to the library and bring home books and magazines that you think might interest him. Then, leave them in a place where they'll readily catch his eye.

As a teacher, I've had many books intended for the classroom on the coffee table in the living room. When my children (one a teenager and the other in grade school) saw the titles, their curiosity prompted them to open the books, and they sat right down and read them to the end.

Some of these books were too easy for them. But they answered questions about the universe or told about a famous person, and my children wanted to get this information. Some were written for teachers. But they described art or science projects that my children wanted to do. So they read the books even though they weren't written for their age levels.

All the subjects—the history of the flag, the causes of the weather, the changes in the calendar, as examples—aroused my children's interest. But my son and daughter seemed to be unaware that books like these existed to tantalize their intellects. They never went to the library and took out books like these on their own.

Then too, if the books were in order on the shelf, they stayed there—neat and organized. But out on the kitchen table right in front of the children when they came for a snack, the words caught their attention, and they opened the books and read.

The same was true for magazines and newspapers. Breakfast included headlines of the morning paper with eye-catching front-page pictures that demanded a verbal explanation. As they ate, the children would read the article that told about the picture. When a new *Time* or *Sports Illustrated* came, I would put it in a prominent place. On those days, my son never failed to grab it and start to read when he came home from school.

But if the newspapers and magazines piled up in an uninteresting clutter, they lost their appeal. The children seemed to be tempted to look at one or two magazines but not to burrow through a stack to find one that struck their interest. Then too, the freshness of a current issue with timely news had an influence on their motivation to read.

One way to combine timeliness with a more personal motivational force is to give your child book-club and magazine subscriptions as gifts. When he gets his own mail, he wants to examine it right away. He'll get involved with the book or magazine because it's his. At the same time, you're sharing your love of reading with him by telling him that this is a fun way to spend time and money. When he reads the material from month to month, he'll come to the same conclusion.

Suggestions for book clubs and appropriate children's magazine subscriptions can be obtained at the library. Nancy Larrick's *A Parent's Guide to Reading* and May Hill Arbuthnot's *Children's Reading in the Home* will give you other ideas.

You can also find a good selection of paperback books and magazines at the drugstore and the supermarket. Maybe your child will be hooked into a series like the *Hardy Boys* or *Nancy Drew*. Maybe he'll like a magazine with puzzles, stories, poems, riddles, and activities to entertain him. Even comic books can stimulate an interest in reading. They'll also give the message that it's fun to read.

And don't overlook adult books. Once your child is in fourth grade, his interests mirror yours. He can build his skills and enjoy many books that are written for a mass market. My son never sat and read for hours at a time the way I did. He didn't particularly like fiction. But he liked to read factual accounts of other people's lives and informative books like *The Guiness Book of World Records*. Adult books frequently satisfied his need for information.

Also, remember to be aware of your child's interests when you choose—or help him choose—his reading material. When my son was in fifth and sixth grade, he loved football. He read magazines that gave information about the players and statistics about the teams. He read the sports page of the daily newspaper. He read books about the players and coaches, such as *Star Running Backs of the NFL* by Bill Libby and *Instant Replay* by Jerry Kramer.

His reading pattern through the years from eleven to fifteen followed his interests. He went from football to motorcycles, from camping to cars. In between, he read about the care and training of dogs and the dangers of drugs. His books taught him how to play pool, how to collect beer cans, and how to make his own fudge. As his interests changed, his reading changed.

To encourage those interests, I surrounded him with reading in those subjects. Whenever I went to the library, I would bring a book or magazine home that answered some of his current questions or expanded his knowledge in a new way. For his birthday, I always included a book among his gifts. I gave him his own subscription to *Sports Illustrated* so that each week he would look forward to reading that magazine. I wanted him to include reading in his daily routine.

In short, then, if you have a variety of timely, readable printed matter in your home, your child will read it. But he won't read as much or as willingly unless he has a restful setting and the time to read. So give him a quiet atmosphere. See to it that he has few distractions so he can concentrate and absorb what he reads.

Turn the television off

According to the last census, 98 percent of the homes in the United States have television sets and the average family watches four to six hours of TV every night. This means that from the time a child comes home from school until he goes to bed, he hears and sees something on the screen. Even if he doesn't watch it himself, he's constantly distracted by it.

He doesn't have a chance to think about or decide what he'd like to do next. Too often, he just sits down and lets himself be entertained. At the time in his life when he should add to his skills in reading or be active in sports or be engaged in a creative endeavor, he interacts with a television set. Television programs fill up his time.

In fact, they fill up more of his time than school does. The average child between the ages of five and eighteen watches approximately 16,000 hours of TV, but he spends only 12,000 hours in school. We know that those school hours consist of many activities that don't require him to read. So if we want to make sure he has success in school, we must see to it that he reads at home.

We're reluctant to do that, though. We don't want to decide for our child how he should spend his free time; we want him to be independent, to make his own decisions. We want him to turn the set off on his own and find other ways to amuse himself. But whether we realize it or not, if we keep the TV on all the time, we don't give him a fair choice; we've made the decision for him. If he watches television, he can't read. He can't do both at the same time.

As parents, we must make a *conscious* decision about what we want to teach our children. We must guide them to other recreational activities besides television. We must decide not to use television as a babysitter. We must avoid giving our children the message that TV is the most fun they can have by forbidding them to watch when they don't do well in school or when we want to punish them. We must regulate the amount of television that they watch so they can develop their minds and bodies in healthy ways.

When I took the television out of the kitchen and the living room of my home and made those family areas into quiet communication centers, I saw an increase in talking and reading. My children didn't want to sit and watch television alone. They didn't want to be isolated away from the family. They came to be with me while I prepared a meal. They came to sit with me while I read.

When the house was quiet, they thought about how to spend their free time. I made them tell me what their plans were for the next hour. I made them think of several possibilities and decide which one would be most satisfying.

They began to look at the television guide and think of the programs as only one of their options instead of as their way of life. I limited the amount of time they could watch television, and they had to choose the programs they liked best. If I didn't agree that their selection was appropriate, I told them why and made them defend their choice.

If they had nothing else to do, they started to look around and read some of the materials I had provided. Without the constant sound of the television, they could appreciate the entertainment that reading offered. They began to see that they enjoyed a book or magazine more than the "Flintstones" or "Gilligan's Island."

I began to see an interesting pattern evolve. When my children looked for new ways to spend their free time, they read more. And when they read, they got new ideas for ways to spend their free time. When she was young, Jennifer followed the activities of *Big Bird's Busy Book, Richard Scarry's Best Rainy Day Book Ever,* and the *Tell It-Make It Book* by Shari Lewis. As she grew older, she made some of the recipes from *Betty Crocker's Cookbook for Boys and Girls* and taught herself the sign language of the deaf when she read *The Helen Keller Story.* She learned to utilize her own time in constructive ways through books.

So decide what you want for your child. Decide what kind of messages you give him every day. Do you really encourage him to read? When you turn your television off, you can be sure you're creating an atmosphere that will promote reading in your home.

Expect your child to read every day

If you think your child should read, he will. You'll set his growth in reading as a priority in your own life. You'll keep this goal in mind and take steps to achieve it.

You'll direct your child to read when he has odd moments before dinner or before he goes out for some activity. You'll make sure reading is a regular part of his free time.

You'll set aside a specific time to read together. It may begin as individual skill development when you teach your child to read or help him improve in reading. It may be as a family when everyone agrees to have a quiet hour to read. It may be your child's own time that he designates to read for school book reports or social studies or science assignments.

You'll notice when he reads on his own. You'll create an atmosphere that encourages him to read at those times. For example, if he's inclined to read when he comes home from school, you'll see that the house is quiet for him then.

You'll be aware of what he reads. You'll mentally record his interests and look for printed matter that reflects them. You'll bring home magazines and books that arouse his curiosity. You'll find articles in your own reading and call his attention to them.

You'll take him to the library so he can select materials on his own that satisfy his desire to acquire information. You'll take the time to help him find suitable books and magazines.

You'll praise him for his efforts and show an interest when he tells you about what he's read. Your smiles and positive feedback will add to his own good feelings about his experiences with reading.

You'll observe *how* he reads. You'll have him read aloud to you at intervals to check on his progress in reading. You'll ask his teacher to tell you about his understanding of school texts. You'll help him when you listen to him read.

And once he's reading every day, you'll see him accumulate knowledge gradually and steadily. You'll observe that he can express himself more clearly in speech and in writing. You'll hear new vocabulary and more articulate language patterns. You'll note that he's able to finish his own work and that he's doing better in school.

He, in turn, will begin to think of reading as a way to solve his problems as well as to entertain himself. And when he enjoys reading, he'll want to read more. He'll develop the pattern to become a lifelong reader.

You'll have accomplished your goal.

Appendix **1**

Recommended learning toys

This appendix lists all the toys and records I've mentioned in this book and gives a brief description of each. It's divided into two major parts: Preschool and Beginning Reading. Each of these parts is divided into smaller categories that, I hope, will make it easy for you to find any item you're looking for.

Most of the items listed are followed by either a *T*, an *S*, or an *O* in parentheses that tells you where to find the item. The *T* stands for toy, variety, drug, and department stores; the *S* stands for school-supply stores; and the *O* means you have to order directly from the manufacturer. The first two categories are not mutually exclusive; I've simply used them to show where I've found each item to be most readily available.

PRESCHOOL

Art Materials, Clay, and Stencils (T)

Fisher-Price Art Kit #700	Set has watercolors and water tray, safety scissors, glue, a 6″ ruler, 5 colored chalks, 16 crayons, 3 geometric shape stencils, construction paper, 2 magnets, and an idea booklet, all in a durable plastic storage case with handle.

Art Materials, Clay, and Stencils (continued)

The Scribbler's inexpensive sets of art materials (made by Western Publishing Co., Inc.) give a child many opportunities to experiment with colors, stencils, clay, etc.:

The Scribbler's Play Tray with Markers	19 different-sized geometric and shape stencils with a plastic tray and 6 wide-tip colored marker pens.
The Scribbler's Play Tray with Modeling Clay	4 plastic geometric cutters (circle, square, diamond, and triangle) with a plastic tray and 4 sticks of clay.
The Scribbler's Simple Shape Stencils	6 stencil cards with shapes in many sizes, 6 crayons, a pencil, and paper.

Blocks, Beads, Pegboards, and Play Tiles

Attribute Blocks (S):

Invicta Plastics Ltd. #NV1107	Set contains a total of 60 blocks; there are 5 different geometric shapes, each in 2 thicknesses, 3 colors, and 2 sizes.

Beads and Pattern Cards (T):

Playskool #702	28 jumbo wooden beads in 4 shapes and 4 colors with 2 laces.
Playskool #7043	20 pattern cards.

Cube Blocks and Pattern Cards (S):

Playskool #302	25 colored wood cubes; pattern sheet included.
Playskool #7042	20 pattern cards.

Geometric Blocks (T):

Playskool #640	36 natural wood blocks in 7 shapes.
Playskool #646	49 wood blocks in 7 shapes and 6 colors (blue, yellow, purple, red, orange, and green).

Lego Blocks (T):

Plastic interlocking building pieces with pattern ideas and board. Many sets available.

#333	For ages 3–5; contains 91 pieces.

Loc Blocs (T):

Preschool or regular size interlocking building blocks in a variety of shapes, sizes, and colors. (Made by Entex Industries, Inc.)

#1042	Giant preschool set with 100 pieces.
#1067	16-piece set.
#1089	70-piece set.

Parquetry Blocks and Pattern Cards (S):

Playskool #306	32 colored wood parquetry blocks of various shapes; 4 pattern cards.
Playskool #7020	20 pattern cards.

Pegboards (T):

Lauri, Inc. #2441	8″ square pegboard of crepe foam rubber comes with 25 large colored pegs.
Lauri, Inc. #2440	11-1/2″ square pegboard of crepe foam rubber comes with 25 large and 40 small colored pegs.

Play Tiles (T):

Playskool #436

35 pieces in 5 shapes and 5 colors make geometric designs and creative pictures with a pegboard. Easy.

Mr. Mighty Mind

32 colorful geometric wood shapes and 30 basic activity cards with patterns numbered according to level of difficulty. Preschool. (Made by Leisure Learning Products, Inc.)

Mr. Super Mind

32 colorful geometric wood shapes and 30 activity cards with patterns of varying difficulty. For the more advanced child. (Made by Leisure Learning Products, Inc.)

Pyramid Blocks (T):

Child Guidance #590

Learning tower.

Playskool #1071

Stacking drums of different colors and sizes.

Playskool #1073

Stacking barrels; 5 barrels (10 pieces) come apart and fit inside each other.

Chalkboards (T)

Child Guidance #53100 Magnetic Muppet Board

20″ x 13″ magnetized chalkboard with handle and legs. Set includes chalk, eraser, and magnetic Sesame Street muppets to hold notes to any metal surface. All the uppercase letters are printed across the top of the board and all the lowercase letters are printed across the bottom as a guide for printing.

Chalkboards (continued)

Child Guidance #51011
Pack 'n Go Chalkboard

An inexpensive, durable, colorful, 13″ square portable chalkboard with handle and storage. Comes with chalk and eraser and has capital letters A-M printed on the left side and N-Z printed on the right side of the board.

Playskool #554
Draw 'n Spell Desk

A portable lap desk that includes a magnetic chalkboard with storage for the chalk, eraser, and 26 uppercase magnetic letters that come with it.

Lotto Games (T)

Edu-Cards: Each set has six boards and 36 cover cards.

#E100   ABC
#E101   Zoo
#E104   Farm
#E115   World Around Us
#E120   What's Missing
#E121   Go Together Lotto
#E127   Object Lotto

Puzzles

Number Puzzle (S):

Lauri, Inc. #2307

10 numbers fit into a colorful 11-1/2″ square board; all made of crepe foam rubber.

Picture Puzzles (T):

Playskool woodboard are graded First, Easy, and Storybook. My favorites are as follows:

First:	#180-04	Things with Wheels—4 pieces.
	#180-10	Vegetables—4 pieces.
	#180-11	Water Pals—4 pieces.
Easy:	#186-04	Picnic—7 pieces.
	#186-06	Bluebirds—6 pieces.
	#186-07	Horse—5 pieces.
	#186-08	Squirrel—5 pieces.
Storybook:	#290-07	Hansel and Gretel—11 pieces.
	#290-08	Little Red Riding Hood—12 pieces.

Shape Puzzle (S):

Lauri, Inc. #2101	Colorful shapes fit into crepe rubber boards. Use also as stencils.

Sequence Cards (S)

Milton Bradley #7547	12 sets, each with 4 scene sequences.
Milton Bradley #7548	6 sets, each with 8 scene sequences.
Milton Bradley #7549	4 sets, each with 12 scene sequences.

Records

Tom Glazer: CMS Records, Inc.

#657	"Activity and Game Songs, Vol. 1"
#658	"Activity and Game Songs, Vol. 2"
#687	"Activity and Game Songs, Vol. 3"

Records (continued)

Ella Jenkins: Folkway Records and Service Corporation

#FC 7543   "My Street Begins at My House"
#FC 7652   "This is Rhythm"
#FC 7660   "Nursery Rhymes"
#SC 7680   "Rhythm and Game Songs for the Little Ones"

Pete Seeger: Folkway Records and Service Corporation

#FC 7601   "American Folk Songs for Children"

BEGINNING READING

To Teach the Names of the Letters

Alphabet Blocks (T):

Playskool #226	16 wood blocks with letters embossed and printed on 4 sides with non-toxic colors.
Playskool #214	30 wood blocks as above.

Alphabet Puzzles (S):

Letters fit into colorful 11-1/2″ square boards made of crepe foam rubber.

Lauri, Inc. #2305	26 uppercase letters.
Lauri, Inc. #2306	26 lowercase letters.

Alphabet Stencils (T):

The Scribbler's Bag of Letters	26 inexpensive, colorful, cardboard, 4″ uppercase letters, pre-cut for tracing. (Made by Western Publishing Company, Inc.)

Magnetic Alphabet Board (T):

Fisher-Price #673

On one side, each magnetized plastic letter has its own place in a tray. The reverse side is a metal spelling board. Use as a puzzle or make words with the letters.

Magnetic Letters (T):

Use on magnetic chalkboards, refrigerator, or any metal surface. Plastic alphabet made with circles and straight lines guides your child to print the same way.

Child Guidance #53406

36 uppercase letters with built-in magnets.

Child Guidance #53407

39 lowercase letters with built-in magnets.

Wooden Letters (S):

Your child can trace these letters and, later, use them to make words.

Instructo Corp. #1231

4″ uppercase letters.

Instructo Corp. #1233

4″ lowercase letters.

To Teach Letters and Sounds (O)

Mike Murach & Assoc., Inc. Letter-Sound Cards for Pre-Readers

52 flash cards—26 are alphabet cards with the uppercase letter on one side and the lowercase letter on the other; the other 26 have a picture and word for each letter on one side with several words that start with the same letter on the other side.

To Teach Words (O)

Mike Murach & Assoc., Inc. Word Cards for Beginning Readers	100 flash cards of beginning sight words and word patterns (those given in figures 8-6, 8-7, and 8-8 of this book).
Mike Murach & Assoc., Inc. Word Cards for Advanced Readers	100 flash cards of more advanced word patterns (those given in figure 9-2 of this book).

TOY AND RECORD MANUFACTURERS

Most toy, school-supply, and record stores are happy to order items for you if they don't have them in stock. So here are the manufacturers of all the learning toys and records I've listed above, in case you want to ask your local store owner to order any of them.

Child Guidance
Gabriel Industries
New York, NY 10010

Learning Tower (pyramid blocks)
Magnetic Letters
Magnetic Muppet Board
Pack 'n Go Chalkboard

CMS Records, Inc.
New York, NY 10007

Tom Glazer's Records

Edu-Cards
KPB Industries
Bethlehem, PA 18017

Lotto Games

Entex Industries, Inc.
Compton, CA 90220

Loc Blocs (plastic interlocking blocks)

Fisher-Price
East Aurora, NY 14052

Art Kit
Magnetic Alphabet Board

Folkway Records and
Service Corp.
New York, NY 10023

Ella Jenkins' Records
Pete Seeger's Records

Instructo Corp.
Malvern, PA 19355

Wooden Letters

Invicta Plastics Ltd.
New York, NY 10011

Attribute Blocks

Lauri, Inc.
Phillips-Avon, ME 04966

Alphabet, Number, and Shape Puzzles
Pegboards

Lego Systems, Inc.
Enfield, CT 06082

Lego Blocks (plastic interlocking
    blocks)

Leisure Learning
Products Inc.
Greenwich, CT 06830

Mr. Mighty Mind (play tiles)
Mr. Super Mind (play tiles)

Milton Bradley
Springfield, MD 01115

Sequence Cards

Playskool, Inc.
Chicago, IL 60651

Alphabet Blocks
Beads and Pattern Cards
Cube Blocks and Pattern Cards
Draw 'n Spell Desk
Geometric Blocks
Parquetry Blocks and Pattern Cards
Play Tiles
Puzzles
Stacking Barrels and Drums (pyramid
    blocks)

Western Publishing
Co., Inc.
Racine, WI 53404

The Scribbler's Bag of Letters
The Scribbler's Play Trays
The Scribbler's Shape Stencils

The following are not available in local stores. They must be ordered directly from the publisher:

Mike Murach &
Associates, Inc.
4222 W. Alamos
Suite 101
Fresno, CA 93711

Letter-Sound Cards
Word Cards

Appendix **2**

Books to delight your child

PRESCHOOL: TO READ TO YOUR CHILD

Picture Books

Baby's First ABC (Platt and Munk, 1960)
Baby's First Counting Book (Platt and Munk, 1960)
Picture Book ABC, Helen Jill Fletcher (Platt and Munk, 1978)

Mother Goose

Mother Goose, Watty Piper, ed. (Platt and Munk, 1972)
Richard Scarry's Best Mother Goose Ever, Richard Scarry (Western Publishing Company, Inc., 1970)

Word Books

My Weekly Reader Picture Word Book, Adelaide Holl (Grosset and Dunlap, 1975)
Richard Scarry's Best Counting Book Ever, Richard Scarry (Random House, 1975)
Richard Scarry's Best Word Book Ever, Richard Scarry (Western Publishing Company, Inc., 1971)

Classics (also available in many other editions)

Cinderella (Random House, 1960)
Complete Adventures of Peter Rabbit (Frederick Warne, 1982)
The Gingerbread Boy, retold and illus. by Paul Galdone (The Seabury Press, 1975)
King Midas and the Golden Touch, Al Perkins (Random House, 1969)
The Little Red Hen, illus. by Paul Galdone (The Seabury Press, 1973)
The Three Bears, ed. and illus. by Paul Galdone (The Seabury Press, 1972)
The Three Billy Goats Gruff, Peter Christen Asbjornsen, illus. by Paul Galdone (The Seabury Press, 1973)
The Three Little Pigs, illus. by Paul Galdone (The Seabury Press, 1970)

New Classics

Norman Bridwell:

Clifford, the Big Red Dog (Four Winds Press, 1963)
Clifford's Good Deeds (Four Winds Press, 1975)

Ezra Jack Keats:

Peter's Chair (Harper and Row, 1967)
The Snowy Day (The Viking Press, 1962)
The Trip (Greenwillow Books, 1978)
Whistle for Willie (The Viking Press, 1964)

Robert McCloskey:

Make Way for Ducklings (The Viking Press, 1969)

Hans Augusto Rey:

Curious George (Houghton Mifflin Company, 1941)
Curious George Learns the Alphabet (Houghton Mifflin Company, 1963)

New Classics (continued)

Bernard Waber:

Lovable Lyle (Houghton Mifflin Company, 1969)
Lyle and the Birthday Party (Houghton Mifflin Company, 1966)
Lyle, Lyle Crocodile (Houghton Mifflin Company, 1965)

Random House: Beginner Books Series

Are You My Mother?, P. D. Eastman, 1960
The Best Nest, P. D. Eastman, 1968
I Wish That I Had Duck Feet, Theo. Le Sieg, 1965
Put Me in the Zoo, Robert Lopshire, 1960

BEGINNING READING BOOKS

To Teach Letters and Sounds

Dr. Seuss's ABC, Dr. Seuss (Random House, 1963)
Richard Scarry's ABC Book, Richard Scarry (Random House, 1971)

To Teach Your Child to Read

Word Book

Richard Scarry's Best Word Book Ever, Richard Scarry (Western Publishing Company, Inc., 1971)

Random House: Beginner Books Series

The Diggingest Dog, Al Perkins, 1967
Go, Dog, Go, P. D. Eastman, 1961
Put Me In The Zoo, Robert Lopshire, 1960
Ten Apples Up On Top, Theo. Le Sieg, 1961

Step-by-Step Reading Program

Programmed Reading (a Sullivan Associates Program), Cynthia Dee Buchanan: 21 books, plus a primer, storybooks, and 3 teacher's guides. Published by the Webster Division of McGraw-Hill, New York, NY 10020.

For More Advanced Readers

Children's Press: The True Book Series

The True Book of Communication, O. Irene Sevrey Miner, 1960
The True Book of Dinosaurs, Mary Lou Clark, 1981
The True Book of Health, Olive V. Haynes, 1954
The True Book of Horses, Elsa Posell, 1961
The True Book of Transportation, Elsa Posell, 1957

Thomas Y. Crowell Company: Biographies

Cesar Chavez, Ruth Franchere, 1970
Jim Thorpe, Thomas Fall, 1970
Malcolm X, Arnold Adoff, 1970
Maria Tallchief, Tobi Tobias, 1970

Thomas Y. Crowell Company: Let's Read and Find Out Science Books

How a Seed Grows, Helene J. Jordan, 1960
The Sun: Our Nearest Star, Franklin M. Branley, 1961
A Tree is a Plant, Clyde Robert Bulla, 1960
What Makes a Shadow, Clyde Robert Bulla, 1962

Harper and Row: I Can Read Series

General:

The Fire Cat, Esther Averill, 1960
Sammy the Seal, Syd Hoff, 1959

Harper and Row: I Can Read Series (continued)

Mystery:

Big Max, Kin Platt, 1977
The Case of the Cat's Meow, Crosby Bonsall, 1965

Science:

Ants are Fun, Mildred Myrick, 1968
Let's Get Turtles, Millicent Selsam, 1965
Seeds and More Seeds, Millicent Selsam, 1959
Terry and the Caterpillars, Millicent Selsam, 1962

Sports:

Here Comes the Strikeout, Leonard Kessler, 1965
Kick, Pass and Run, Leonard Kessler, 1966

Putnam's Sons: See and Read Beginning to Read Biographies

Abraham Lincoln, Patricia Miles Martin, 1964
Christopher Columbus, Helen D. Olds, 1964
George Washington, Vivien L. Thompson, 1964
John Fitzgerald Kennedy, Patricia Miles Martin, 1964

Franklin Watts, Ltd.: Let's Find Out Series

The Easy Book of Division, David C. Whitney, 1970
The Easy Book of Multiplication, David C. Whitney, 1969
Let's Find Out About Addition, David C. Whitney, 1966
Let's Find Out About Subtraction, David C. Whitney, 1968

BOOKS TO KEEP YOUR CHILD READING: GRADE 3 ON

Classics (available in many different editions)

Alice in Wonderland, Lewis Carroll
Big Red, Jim Kjelgaard
The Black Stallion, Walter Farley
The Call of the Wild, Jack London
A Christmas Carol, Charles Dickens
The Complete Fairy Tales and Stories, Hans Christian Andersen
Hans Brinker, Or, The Silver Skates, Mary Mapes Dodge
Heidi, Johanna Spyri
The Little Prince, Antoine de Saint-Exupery
Winnie-the-Pooh, A. A. Milne

Make-and-Do Books

Betty Crocker's Cookbook for Boys and Girls (Golden, 1975)
Big Bird's Busy Book (Random House, 1975)
Richard Scarry's Best Rainy Day Book Ever (Random House, 1974)
Tell It—Make It Book, Shari Lewis (J. P. Tarcher, Inc., 1972)

Mystery Series

Hardy Boys Mystery Stories (Grosset and Dunlap, Inc.)
Nancy Drew Mystery Stories (Simon and Schuster)

Random House: Step-Up Series

Football Players Do Amazing Things, Mel Cebulash, 1975
Magicians Do Amazing Things, Robert Kraske, 1979
Meet John F. Kennedy, Nancy Bean White, 1965

Special Interest

The Guiness Book of World Records, Norris McWhister, ed. (Sterling Publishing Company, Inc., 1980)
The Helen Keller Story, Catherine Owens Peare (Crowell, 1959)
Instant Replay, Jerry Kramer (World Publishing, 1968)
Star Running Backs of the NFL, Bill Libby (Random House, 1971)

GUIDES TO ADDITIONAL BOOKS

Children's Reading in the Home, May Hill Arbuthnot (Scott Foresman and Company, 1969)
A Parent's Guide to Reading—4th Edition, Nancy Larrick (Doubleday and Company, Inc., 1975)

CHILDREN'S DICTIONARY

Webster's Intermediate Dictionary (G. & C. Merriam Co., 1977)

Bibliography

Chapter 1

Bernstein, Basil. *Class, Codes and Control*, Vol. 1. London: Routledge and Kegan Paul Ltd., 1971.

Bulcock, Jeffrey W., Clifton, Rodney A., Beebe, Mona J. "Reading Competency as a Predictor of Scholastic Performance: Comparisons Between Industrialized and Third World Nations" in *Cross-Cultural Perspectives on Reading and Reading Research*, pp. 4-47. Edited by Dina Feitelson. Newark, Delaware: International Reading Association, Inc., 1978.

Coleman, James S., et al. *Report on Educational Opportunity in the United States*. Washington, D. C.: U.S. Government Printing Office, 1966.

Hess, Robert D. and Shipman, Virginia. "Parents as Teachers: How Lower Class and Middle Class Mothers Teach," in *Readings in Child Behavior and Development*, pp. 437-446. Edited by Celia Stendler Lavatelli and Faith Stendler. New York: Harcourt, Brace, Jovanovich, Inc., 1972.

Jencks, Christopher. *Inequality: A Reassessment of the Effect of Family and Schooling in America*. New York: Harper and Row, 1972.

Chapter 3

Durkin, Dolores. *Children Who Read Early*. New York: Teachers College Press, 1966.

Chapter 4

Fisher, Dorothy Canfield. *Montessori for Parents.* Cambridge, Massachusetts: Robert Bentley, Inc., 1940.

Ginsburg, Herbert and Opper, Sylvia. *Piaget's Theory of Intellectual Development: An Introduction.* Englewood Cliffs, N. J.: Prentice-Hall, Inc., 1969.

Montessori, Maria. *The Absorbent Mind.* New York: Holt, Rinehart, and Winston, 1967.

Montessori, Maria. *The Montessori Method.* New York: Schocken Books, 1964.

Orem, R. C., ed. *A Montessori Handbook.* New York: G. P. Putnam's Sons, 1966.

Phillips, John L., Jr. *The Origins of Intellect: Piaget's Theory.* San Francisco: W. H. Freeman and Co., 1969.

Index

217

3 sets of flash cards
to help your child become a good reader

All created by Nancy L. Johnson,
author of *How to Insure Your Child's Success in School*

Letter-Sound Cards
for Pre-Readers

52 flash cards that give your child a solid foundation for reading.

The first 26 are alphabet cards. They have the uppercase letter on one side and the lowercase letter on the other.

The second 26 are letter-sound cards. On the front side, they have a letter, a picture of a word that starts with that letter, and the word that identifies the picture. On the back are additional words that start with the same letter and sound.

These cards will teach your child:

- the letters of the alphabet ... both upper and lowercase so he or she can recognize them no matter how they're written
- one common sound for each letter
- how to sound out simple words that follow the regular letter-sound relationships
- how to start writing the letters
- how to listen for the sounds in words ... a prerequisite to becoming a good speller
- that you read words starting with the letters at the left and moving to the right
- that the words you say can also be written down and read by you or someone else later on
- that learning the letters and sounds is special and fun ... like knowing a secret code

Complete instructions are included to show you how to use the cards effectively with your child. Or you can follow the suggestions in chapter 8 of *How to Insure Your Child's Success in School*.

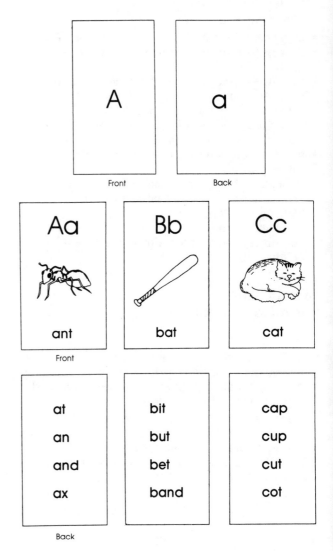

**More about the card sets
on the other side** ⟶

Word Cards
for Beginning Readers

100 flash cards of many often-used words to teach your child to read.

The cards fall into two groups. One group has a word beginning with a small letter on one side and the same word starting with a capital letter on the other side. The second group has a root word on one side and additional words that follow the same pattern on the other side.

These cards teach your child:

- to recognize common words ... no matter where they appear in a sentence or whether they're capitalized
- that when you put one or two letters before a word or when you change the first letter of the word, you make a new word
- to see the little words in bigger words, so he or she can begin to figure out unfamiliar words
- to sound out words that follow regular letter-sound patterns
- to begin to recognize some common words that are irregular and can't be sounded out (words like *you* and *the*)
- to assign sounds not only to single letters but also to regular combinations of letters (like *th*, *bl*, etc.)

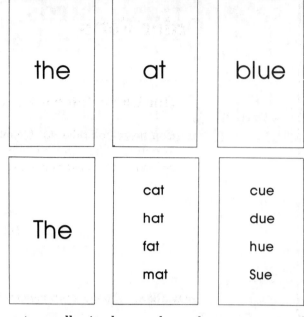

- to spell simple words and common sound patterns
- that you read starting with the letters at the left and moving to the right

Complete instructions are included to show you how to use the cards effectively with your child. Or you can follow the suggestions in chapter 8 of *How to Insure Your Child's Success in School.*

Word Cards
for Advanced Readers

100 flash cards that teach your child to be a fluent reader. You can use them either to enhance the skills of a child in the primary grades or to do remedial work with an older child.

Each card has a basic sound pattern on one side. On the other side are words that use that pattern. Some of the patterns are found most often at the beginning of words, some in the middle of words, and some are word endings.

These cards will teach your child:

- to respond automatically with a sound to common word patterns
- to break large, unfamiliar words down into word patterns he or she recognizes and can read
- to learn common patterns that don't follow the regular letter-sound relationships (like *su* in *treasure* and *usual*)
- to recognize that a change in the beginning, middle, or end of a word affects its pronunciation and meaning (for example, the verb *confide* becomes the noun *confidence* when the *ence* ending is added)
- to look carefully at each letter in the word

- to use the word patterns whenever he or she is reading
- to spell the word patterns correctly

Complete instructions are included to show you how to use the cards effectively with your child. Or you can follow the suggestions in chapter 9 of *How to Insure Your Child's Success in School.*

 Mike Murach & Associates, Inc. • 4222 W. Alamos, Suite 101 • Fresno, CA 93711 • 209-275-3335

Order Form

Our Unconditional Guarantee

You must be satisfied. If you ever feel that our products aren't effective, you can return them for a full and immediate refund ... no questions asked.

Mike Murach, President
Mike Murach and Associates, Inc.

fold   fold

Dear Mike: Please send me the following items.

Quantity	Item	Description	Price
_____	Book	*How to Insure Your Child's Success in School*, 219 pages	$15.00
_____	Card set 1	*Letter-Sound Cards for Pre-Readers*, 52 flash cards plus instructions (cards measure 5¾" x 3½")	5.50
_____	Card set 2	*Word Cards for Beginning Readers*, 100 flash cards plus instructions (cards measure 5¾" x 3½")	5.50
_____	Card set 3	*Word Cards for Advanced Readers*, 100 flash cards plus instructions (cards measure 5¾" x 3½")	5.50

☐ I have enclosed my check or money order for full payment. I understand each price includes shipping and handling charges in the U.S. (California residents, please add 6% sales tax to your order total.)

☐ Charge the products (and sales tax, if applicable) to my
_____ Visa _____ MasterCard:

Card number _____ Valid thru (mo/yr) _____

Cardowner's signature _____
(not valid without signature)

Name _____

Street Address _____

City, State, Zip _____

fold   fold

Fold where indicated and staple.

No postage necessary if mailed in the United States.

Comment Form

Your opinions count

Your opinions today will affect our products and policies of tomorrow. So if you have questions, criticisms, or suggestions, I'm eager to get them. You can expect a response within a week of when we receive your comments.

Also, if you discover any errors in this book, typographical or otherwise, please point them out. We'll correct them when the book is reprinted.

Thanks for your help!

Mike Murach, President
Mike Murach and Associates, Inc.

Book title: How to Insure Your Child's Success in School

Dear Mike: _____

_____

_____

_____

_____

_____

_____

_____

_____

_____

_____

_____

_____

_____

_____

_____

_____

_____

Name _____

Street Address _____

City, State, Zip _____

Fold where indicated and staple.
No postage necessary if mailed in the United States.

fold   fold

BUSINESS REPLY MAIL

First Class   Permit No. 3063   Fresno, CA

NO POSTAGE
NECESSARY
IF MAILED
IN THE
UNITED STATES

POSTAGE WILL BE PAID BY ADDRESSEE

Mike Murach & Associates, Inc.

4222 West Alamos, Suite 101

Fresno, California 93711

fold   fold